OUTSOURCING VERSUS OFFSHORING

BUSINESS AND PSYCHOLOGY PERSPECTIVES

DR. IVAN J. SALABERRIOS

Pensiero Press

Outsourcing versus Offshoring

Pensiero Press

Websites: www.ThePensieroPress.com | www.LentzLeadership.com
Twitter: https://twitter.com/drcheryllentz
Facebook: https://www.facebook.com/Dr.Cheryl.Lentz

Books are available through Pensiero Press at special discounts for bulk purchases for the purpose of sales promotion, seminar attendance, or educational purposes.

Volume ISBN: 978-1-7329382-7-4

LAW009000 LAW / Business & Financial
*Kindle and electronic versions available

Cover design & production: Gary Rosenberg • www.garyarosenberg.com

Volume 1

AIM TECHNICAL CONSULTANTS

CONTENTS

ABSTRACT

Offshoring remains one of the most heated topics of economic policy of the last three decades. Most debates focus on the drivers of offshoring and the overreaching negative effects of offshoring on the home countries of multinational enterprises. Critics of offshoring see offshoring as a potential threat to the economies of advanced countries, and a threat to long-term competitiveness and innovative capacities of advanced countries. Critics also blame offshoring for the weakening of the manufacturing industry, erosion of domestic capabilities of advanced countries, as well as job losses.

In contrast, pro-offshoring, see offshoring as a source of competitive advantage, as a useful tool to achieve productivity and cost-savings, and as a useful tool for reorganization. It is unclear whether unbiased evidence exists to support the view that offshoring is a threat to the economies of advanced countries and a threat to long-term competitiveness and innovative capacities of advanced countries. Similarly, it is unclear whether there is unbiased evidence to support the pro-offshoring view that offshoring practices should be continued for reasons discussed here. These raging debates in the media and elsewhere continue to influence research on the topic of offshoring in relation to its impacts and drivers. However, mixed results reported in this study increase difficulty for policy makers to determine which way to go: advocate for offshoring or dismiss altogether. This book clears this confusion by elucidating on the drivers of offshoring by taking the business and psychology perspectives. The book further includes review of the results of studies on the effects of offshoring to highlight keynote results in relation to the effects of offshoring. The aim is to dispel any myth not supported by evidence regarding the potential negative effects of offshoring.

PROLOGUE

Introduction

Before Barrack Obama assumed office as the President of the United States in 2008, he made pronouncements on outsourcing that raised concerns among proponents of the Business Process Outsourcing (BPO) industry and others. Obama's pronouncements were largely interpreted in news reports as suggesting that he intended to introduce relevant legislative policies to discourage outsourcing arrangements with a view to protecting jobs for Americans. However, as it turned out, President Obama's plan was to discourage offshoring arrangements rather than outsourcing arrangements. Obama's position on offshoring arrangements was arguably informed by the widely publicized controversial subject of offshoring and its implications in the public debate.

This debate may have been ignited by the publication of the 2004 President's Economic Report, and the European Union (EU) Constitution referendum debate, largely hyped as a French no-vote Referendum. A 2006 Survey of the Australian Parliamentary Library database of Australian newspaper articles, and 2005 Parliamentary Library research briefs on pros and cons of offshoring, fueled the people's concern regarding the negative implications of offshoring on developed country's productivity, employment, innovation, and economies. This debate was further fueled by statistics showing the high number of American and United Kingdom (UK) companies engaging in outsourcing and offshoring activities, including Nike, Caterpillar, and others. Indeed, emerging business practices facilitated by advanced telecommunications and information technologies enabled multinational firms to increasingly engage in offshoring.

The commonly offshored services include back-end management software applications, remote operations of call centers, high-tech research work; and knowledge work (e.g., research and development (Aron & Singh, 2005; Borzo, 2004; Farrell, 2003; Gopal et al., 2003; Horvit, 2004; Slack & Lewis, 2002;). Commonly offshored research and development tasks include software development and maintenance and numerical analysis studies (Farrell, 2003; Horvit, 2004). As revealed in the worldwide survey involving 104 executives from technologic-driven industries in advanced countries, about 70% of the firms employ Research and Development (R & D) talent abroad with 52% of the firms projected to increase their investment in R & D offshored services within the next 4 years (Autor, Dorn, & Hanson, 2013). According to Autor, Dorn, and Hanson (2013), offshoring was projected to be sustained into the 2020s.

The arguments for increased offshoring of technological development, services, and manufacturing vary, ranging from cost-savings to competitive advantage to increased productivity. For Farrell (2005), the overarching argument for offshoring services, technological developing, and manufacturing is to facilitate the optimization of global production, which in turn translates into lower costs, round-the-clock shifts, expanded markets, creation of new opportunities for new entry and existing firms, and lower prices for consumers. This argument remains an empirical question, as well as a highly debated subject for both the policymakers and the public. This debate faces renewed vigor as the United States renegotiates its trade deals with emerging economies such as China and Mexico.

This book delves into these debates by highlighting and including discussion of various forms of offshoring arrangements and models. The book also offers debates on the business and psychological perspective to offshoring taking the empirical and theoretical perspective. The book further offers analysis of the effects of offshoring as documented in the extant literature.

The rest of the book is structured as follow. The first chapter provides the definitions for the key terminologies. Chapter 2 includes discussion of various forms of offshoring and outsourcing. Chapter 3 includes description of the global trends in offshoring and outsourcing. Chapter 4 delves into the negative and positive impacts of offshoring and outsourcing as reflected in the empirical and theoretical studies. Chapter 5 presents the motivators and drivers of offshoring and outsourcing, taking into consideration theoretical and empirical perspectives, as well as taking the business and psychology perspectives. Chapter 6 provides policy responses. Chapter 7 provides a conclusion with policy recommendations. Chapter 8 goes into details about driving productivity with offshoring. Chapter 9 provides insight to the effects of offshoring on the labor market. Chapter 10 includes description of how innovation emerges when properly managing offshore staff. Chapter 11 compares various types of offshoring to back-shoring. Chapter 12 provides a thorough research perspective in the drivers of back-shoring.

CHAPTER 1.
DEFINING OUTSOURCING AND OFFSHORING

Outsourcing

Though the precise definition of offshoring, also known as business process outsourcing (BPO), sub-serving, or outsourcing, is not agreed upon, researchers and experts consistently use these terms to collectively and interchangeably refer to the process of contracting out a business function previously performed in-house to a third-party of external provider (Manning, Massini, & Lewin, 2008). This way of conceptualizing offshoring and outsourcing as one and the same thing has caused considerable confusion. Although the principles between these two terms (i.e., outsourcing and offshoring) are similar, they refer to slightly different things and have different implications and repercussions.

Outsourcing, as used in the popular press and the academic literature, refers to a strategy used by companies that involves contracting services of a third-party service provider or external agency to manage a specific project or set of business processes. In this sense, outsourcing may be said to occur when two companies enter into a contractual agreement that involves the exchange of payments and services, with one firm allowing an external firm to handle its functions. In this way, outsourcing does not involve the physical transfer of assets rather the delegation or assignment of services to another third-party service provider located in another country or region.

Palugod (2011) emphasized that the outsourcing arrangement allows another company to perform some functions of another company previously undertaken in-house or internally. For example, a company can enter an outsourcing arrangement with another company allowing it to manage its, production processes, or finance and payroll services. According to Palugod, an outsourcing arrangement, as used today, refers to the outsourcing of business process and Information Technology (IT) services or the transfer of operational services, rather than manufacturing processes with an aim of reducing services supplied internally and shortening the supply chain. Palugod added that most companies engage in an outsourcing arrangement because they are vertically integrated to perform their IT and business processes. Palugod believed that the aim of outsourcing is to save fixed, production, and development costs often achieved by the company focusing on strengthening its R & D.

Other related terms are *the fragmentation of global value chain, international insourcing, international outsourcing, trade in tasks, international outsourcing,* and *global production sharing* which all describe the location of various stages of production processes (Stehrer et al., 2012).

Outsourcing: The Business and Academic Perspective

Offshoring, as used in the business world and the academic literature, refers to the business' ability to outsource to other companies located in another country (Manning et al., 2008). This suggests that in offshoring, the emphasis is on the relocation of operating activities to another country. Supporting this view, Sethupathy (2013) advanced that offshoring involves a company undertaking a service process or function in a foreign country. In this business arrangement, the function may be undertaken by another company, a subsidiary of the company located in another country, also referred to as shared service division or a captive company. The function or process can be termed both *outsourced* and *offshored* when it is performed by a third-party company. In view of these perspectives, offshoring and outsourcing refer to different yet related processes.

Other related terms have emerged that capture the different aspects of the complex relationship between networks and economic organizations including offshore outsourcing; strategic outsourcing; multi-sourcing; far-shoring, and nearshoring (Manning et al., 2008; Norwood et al., 2006).

Nearshoring is a subdivision of offshoring used to refer to the practice of transferring or outsourcing information technology processes to less expensive companies located in a country that shares the geographical border with the target company. In multi-sourcing, the target company contracts or procures IT operations and technology infrastructure to multiple vendors in combination with the elements of IT provided internally.

Far shoring is a special form of offshoring which involves transferring or outsourcing information technology processes to less expensive companies located in far from the country target company. This form of offshoring is the direct opposite of nearshoring.

Onshoring-the opposite of offshoring is the practice of relocating business processes or functions to a lower-cost location within the country's national borders. The concept behind onshoring is that relocating business processes or functions near customers may foster the establishment of closer working agreements and facilitate the faster provision of services that are tailored to suite market needs. It is also argued that through onshoring, a company can improve its cost structure, foster flexibility, and improve communication and coordination of production.

Offshore outsourcing as used in this book refers to **the strategic practice involving a company or firm contracting a third-party supplier to undertake the work in another or foreign country**.

CHAPTER 2. FORMS OF OFFSHORING AND OUTSOURCING

Several forms of outsourcing have been identified and documented in the extant literature (Javalgi, Joseph, Granot, & Gross, 2013). These forms of offshore outsourcing include IT outsourcing, manufacturing outsourcing, business process outsourcing, process-specific outsourcing, operational outsourcing service, and professional service outsourcing (Javalgi et al., 2013).

Information Technology Outsourcing

As defined by Loh and Venkatraman (1992), IT outsourcing involves partial or full outsourcing of IT functions, including traditional outsourced services and high-end services. These traditional and high-end outsourced IT services and IT processes include change management; operations; managed security; help desk; system integration; application development and maintenance; independent testing and validation; infrastructure management; R & D; cloud computing; and data center management.

Application Development and Maintenance

A company can outsource development and specific modules or functionalities within a software application by allowing the third-party software development company with experiential knowledge and technical skills to address technical specifications. Infrastructure management services that can be outsourced include maintaining overall infrastructure performance, network management, disaster recovery capabilities and strategies, restoring and backing up services, maintaining databases, and troubleshooting errors. Other IT services that can be outsourced include value-added services, performing of downtime analyses, monitoring of IT capacity management and IT infrastructure activities, and reporting of critical system failures.

Help Desk Services

Help desk service commonly outsourced by many companies, include any maintenance service: production support; troubleshooting problems, and infrastructure management. Under this arrangement, the client receives support from the service provider's personnel through various IT problems. An organization can also outsource testing and validation of software that is developed by an independent third party. This specialized testing system can be used to identity and program problems or errors find solutions and monitor the performance of the system.

Data Center Management

Data center operations that can be outsourced include:

- Software, operating system planning, hardware, procurement, specification, maintenance, procurement upgrades, installation, configuration, and management.
- Continuous monitoring of operational status and performance of the server
- Physical hosting of distributed servers, mainframes, and other IT assets
- Recovery of server systems during disasters
- Restoration and backup
- Application software installation and server builds
- Server and mainframe capacity management, including load balancing, capacity planning, reconfiguration, and tuning.

System Integration

Various functions in a decentralized environment are organized through disparate applications and systems that do not communicate with each other. These decentralized environments require human interventions to facilitate system update, detect erroneous results, data sources, and clear out-of-balance conditions. These system integration services encompass developing modules, scripts, programs or tools to integrate multiple systems and applications. These services can be outsourced from the third party to facilitate seamless communication between existing applications and other system to create a consolidated system.

Research and Development (R & D)

To innovate and adapt to meet market demands and construct and maintain business intelligence databases, organizations opt to outsource R & Ds of different solutions, technologies, systems, and processes. Outsourced research may also involve using third-party vendors to undertake market analysis to help identity the responsiveness and trends of key industry sectors.

Managed Security

Many organizations outsource management security services (MSS), Internet security services, intelligence services, security outsourcing, network security services, security consulting, security management, security assessments, and IT security services. MSS is a service that oversees the security of an organization over its IT infrastructure, user management activities, and data assets. Contract terms for the MSS services may include the use of end-to-end security support and architecture design (design consultation, user provisioning, technical support, and design implementation and consultation), and management of security functions of a system, including firewall monitoring, content filtering, data transmission, intrusion detection and response, network vulnerability assessment, and virus protection.

Cloud Computing

Cloud computing offers scalable and visualized computing resources to businesses. Cloud computing offers storage, computer power, and storage as a service. Resources software and offered dynamically. Types of cloud computing services often outsourced by the business include public cloud, private cloud, community cloud, hybrid cloud, and other services: Infrastructure-as-a-service (IaaS), software-as-a-service (SaaS), or platform-as-a-service (PaaS).

Manufacturing Outsourcing

Manufacturing outsourcing is a strategically important type of outsourcing which involves determining the manufacturing activities to be offered to the third party or outside service provider (Ehie, 2001). Companies tend to use manufacturing outsourcing when seeking to use different firms' production facilities rather than make new manufacturing investments or use production facilities in-house (Ehie, 2001).

Business Process Outsourcing (BPO)

Business process outsourcing (BPO) involves moving the business processes to the external service providers from inside the organization (Trkman, 2010). BPO focuses on services and involves delegating non-core business processes, including the design services / products, managing human resources, physical and financial resources, and information to external service providers. Again, the focus of business process management approach is on the business process rather than on the organization's hierarchical and financial structurers (Kohlbacher & Reijers, 2013). The delegation allows the external service provider to own, administers, and manages BPO (Saxena & Bharadwaj, 2009). Using outsourcing, a BPO client (firm) can concentrate on free limited organizational resources and core competency (Brown & Wilson, 2005). Researchers identified several different classifications of business processes. For example, Harmon

(2003) identified crucial business processes as core processes, management processes, and enabling processes.

For Keen (1997), relevant business processes are those that provide options, create value, and sustain value. According to Keen, these business process classifications are either from the service provider perspective or client perspective. Supporting this view, Click and Duening (2005) hinted that from the client perspective, the business processes are classified as support and critical. Elsewhere, Honess (2003) classified business processes into three categories: business non-core non-critical; business critical non-core; and core business processes. According to Honess, core business processes require the most investment and are therefore seldom outsourced. By contrast, the non-critical non-core and critical business processes can be sourced from the third-party service provider. Process classifications can also be observed from the perspective of the service provider.

From this service provider's perspective, BPO projects are classified based on the type of service / product: front-office processing, back-office processing, and middle-office process (Mehta et al., 2006). Front-office BPO includes technical support services and customer service; middle-office processing includes insurance, utilities, banking, and utility services. Back-office BPO supports human resource (HR) processes, customer service, accounting / finance service, or technical support. Back-office BPO encompasses a couple of business processes that large and small organizations can outsource to third-party organizations that specialize in those areas (Saxena & Bharadwaj, 2009). BPO has several advantages: a) cost reduction and cost restructuring and employment of specialized supplier; (b) changing fixed costs into variable costs; (c) improvement of quality; (d) access to outside expert knowledge; (e) access to scale of economies and standardization; (f) sharing of risks; (g) stimulation of local employment; (h) improving management and handling difficult functions; and (i) starting point for introducing crucial changes in the organization.

Outsourcing Type of Service Delivered

Outsourcing can also be defined based on the type of service delivered and how it is delivered. Five common types of outsourcing can be identified based on the service being delivered and the mode of delivery of the service: staff augmentation, project-based outsourcing, out-tasking outsourcing, managed services, offshoring, and out-tasking.

Staff Augmentation

Not all organizations seek for outsourced help to enable them to focus on other important things by pushing some functions off their plate. Sometimes organizations outsource with a view to getting skilled people but not that necessarily because they lack resources or need services full time. When they do so, companies engage in staff augmentation outsourcing. Companies staff augments by offering add-on services such as support services for expanding the market.

Project-based Outsourcing

Project-based outsourcing applies to organizations with irregular or one-off projects. Often these one-off projects have well-defined deliverables and requirements and low-to-medium complexity. Organizations outsource projects to find a dedicated team to work on the task without causing major disruption in their normal operations.

Contracting out / Out-tasking

Out-tasking approach involves transferring specific services or processes from an organization to the outsourcing partner. This outsourcing business model allows the supplier to perform project-oriented processes. These contracting engagements are considered appropriate for business owners seeking to be in control of the outsourced process and may involve contracting and licensing engagements. In licensing, the buyer obtains permission from another company to use its intellectual property, a product or technology for future purposes. Licensing is commonly used as a transactional method in courseware, social media platform, authoring platform, and delivery platform. Similar to licensing, contracting involves one company obtaining the right to manufacture or use a service or a product from another company. In general, contrasting engagements are time-based as the company incurs financial charges on a yearly, monthly, weekly, daily, or hourly basis. Contrasting engagements are favored in less complex and less strategic engagements notably course delivery and instructional design.

Managed Services

Managed services involve the proactive management of the company's infrastructure or backend office functions by the third party. In general, managed service providers assume all responsibilities for problem solving, monitoring, and handling problems for selected business functions. These managed services may include outsourcing IT functions, daily operations, HR activities, and production support.

Offshoring

Offshore outsourcing model involves a company making an outsourcing arrangement that involves locating its resources in another country. Offshoring allows a company to leverage top talents and skilled workers at area relatively lower price than when done in-house. Offshoring also allows the organization to gain access to their clients, as well as access to new market opportunities.

Conclusion

Outsourcing can take any form, namely professional outsourcing, IT outsourcing, manufacturing outsourcing, and project outsourcing. Outsourcing can also be categorized based on the type of service delivered and how it is delivered. In general, each of the outsourcing categories fit specific use and context. For example, outsourcing manufacturing fits companies that specialize in manufacturing physical products while project manufacturing fits companies that focus on specific projects such as writing an e-book or redesigning a website.

CHAPTER 3. OFFSHORING MODELS / SOURCING MODELS

Models

There are various forms of global sourcing models to include: domestic outsourcing, domestic in-sourcing, offshore outsourcing, re-shoring, and captive models. The distinction between these offshoring models largely depends on whether the function is undertaken by an external vendor, a firm's subsidiary business unit, or an offshore location or by the country in which the firm is located. This chapter includes discussions of these forms of global sourcing models.

Domestic Outsourcing

When producing products or services for final demand, organizations may contract third party firms or choose to undertake certain functions in-house for those functions. Example, a firm may outsource research and development (R & D), manufacturing, accounting, cleaning, and transportation by contracting with other firms or perform them in-house. The change in the mix of the *buy* or *make* decision has been labelled the firm's vertical disintegration, growth of networked production, and the changing of the firm's boundary.

Specifically, domestic outsourcing as used within the global context refers to governmental entities or firms situated in one country entering a contractual engagement with individuals or firms located within the same country for service provision or provision of goods. This way, domestic outsourcing involves a firm contracting with a client organization or another company (third party Company) located in the same country to undertake a certain amount of task, at a certain cost, for a specified period or length of time, and level of service.

This definition captures the concept of outsourcing of functions, which used to be undertaken in-house. Types of contractors include vendors or suppliers of services (e.g., staffing firms and business services), goods (e.g., manufacturing inputs), independent contractors (e.g., independent consultants and freelancers, on-demand platform workers), and franchisees.

In view of this definition, domestic outsourcing can occur at three levels: firm level; workplace/job level, and worker level. At the firm level, domestic outsourcing is characterized by changes in the firm's production. This strategy involves increased use of franchising, independent contractors, and contracting out to other firms. The contracting out of services to other firms can involve both the *off*-site and *on*-site, as well as the use of tempt agencies, subcontractors, and other suppliers, vendors, and staffing firms. Franchising and independent contractors are considered forms of contracting out. At the workplace level, domestic offshoring involves changes in the work organization. Its effects include job quality, wages, workload, benefits, schedules, hours, incidence of wage theft, health and safety, access to promotions, as well as training and job stability (Weil, 2014). At the worker level, domestic offshoring causes changes in worker outcomes. At this level, domestic offshoring affects economic security includes bundling different forms of income-generation work, including generation of work (e.g., on demand gigs & standard jobs), and career mobility (Batt & Hiro, 2009).

Several large manufacturing firms embraced American-based domestic offshoring, including Caterpillar, NCR, Ford, Whirlpool, Google, Apple, Nissan, and others. Several studies acknowledged the increasing trend of domestic outsourcing within the United States, and elsewhere. For example, Dube and Kaplan (2010) used the occupation and industry codes in CPS to analyze domestic outsourcing activities in the United States during the 1983-2000 period and reported an increase in the number of guards and janitors working for organizations that offer labor services to other organizations. Similarly, in the 1979-1987 Wage Survey on outsourcing activities, Abraham and Taylor (1996) reported an increase in the volume of work contracted out for machine maintenance, janitorial, computer and accounting tasks, and drafting and engineering tasks. In another study, Dey, Houseman, and Polivka (2010) examined changes in occupation and industry codes in a program involving occupation employment statistics and reported an increase in the share of workers in janitor, truck driver, computer and security occupations employed in areas that specialize in providing services to other organizations. Similarly, Autor (2003) reported an increase in employment in the provision of temporary help services during the 1980-2000 period. In another study, Berlingieri (2013) opined that the increase in the business services and professional outsourcing constituted 14% of the rise in service employment experienced in the United States. Supporting this view, Weil (2014) provided an overview of domestic offshoring and highlighted multiple examples of positive disruptions in business practices that led to outsourcing of changes in the labour force. In another survey based on the previous Contingent Worker Survey, Katz and Krueger (2016), demonstrated an increase in volumes of workers working in alternative work arrangements from 10.7% to 15.8% between 2005 and 2015. Katz and Krueger observed that about half of the increase in the volume of workers in alternative work arrangement in America was as a result of contracting firms and temporary help work. Result of obtained through the Contingent Worker Survey demonstrates an increase in domestic outsourcing in the United States.

Offshore Outsourcing

Off-shoring encompasses transferring of the firm's activities to other low-cost countries. This form of outsourcing allows the firm to make outsourcing arrangements with vendors operating in another country. This way, offshore outsourcing allows firms to cut costs and concentrate on their core business and ultimately grow their profit margin. Offshore outsourcing also provides the company with the opportunity to source globally and low-cost manufacturing (Schuh et al., 2009). According to Schuh et al. (2009), through offshore outsourcing, a company can find the best partners and suppliers and grow the pool of opportunities.

Subcategories of Offshore Outsourcing

Offshore outsourcing can be sub-categorized into three: on shoring, offshoring, and near shoring. On shoring involves offshoring from a short distance from home or simply home region. The key driver of engaging in on shoring could be that similarity in circumstances between the home country and the target country. Near shoring is a form of offshoring describing the process of offshoring activities in countries that are close to each other culturally and geographically. The key driver may be reduced prices in the target country compared to the home country. Last, offshoring is preferred when dealing with countries that provide for geographical advantage (Schuh et al., 2009). The key driver may be reduced lower prices in the target country than home country (Schuh et al., 2009).

Prevalence of Offshoring Outsourcing

Studies demonstrated the consistent increase in offshoring activities globally and within the United States. For example, Welch and Nayak (1992) noted that offshoring outsourcing became a widespread business practice in the United States in the 1950s and 1960s. According to Welch and Nayak, in the 1950s and 1960s companies turned to offshore outsourcing as a strategy to lower wages for their workers, to gain access to innovation and suppliers, convert fixed costs to variable costs, concentrate on core competencies, and shorten the lead-times for improved productivity, and streamlined operations. Welch and Nayak further argued that the outsourcing trend was further driven by the liberalization of international trade and globalization as a result of fast-developing technology and containerization-tog. According to Welch and Nayak, the international trade enabled companies to access the world's best prices, products, and capabilities and this fostered increased offshore outsourcing activities. Welch and Nayak further noted that outsourcing was also fuelled by the spread of lean manufacture and Just-in-Time

(JIT) philosophies, as these philosophies made the easier for companies to outsource diversified product lines and customized products.

Welch and Nayak (1992) argued that lean production and JIT enabled companies to control costs and shorten lead-times as a result of customization of activities. Supporting this view, Vagadia (2012) opined that outsourcing facilitated the shortening of lead times by facilitating the simultaneous completion of tasks. Further commenting on the upsurge in offshoring activities, Qu and Brocklehurst (2003) advanced that offshore outsourcing activities increasingly became a common business practice in the 1990s and 2000s in response to the Y2K problem. Supporting this view, Bunyaratavej, Hahn, and Doh (2007) hinted that firms from developed countries notably the United Kingdom (UK) and the United States, attempted to respond quickly and inexpensively to the Y2K problem by offshoring their services to less expensive offshoring countries such as the Philippines and India. Cauto et al. (2006) argued that the key drivers of this decision by firms to offshore their services to developing counties were searching for qualified workers and labour arbitrage. Cauto et al. further advanced that the success of these offshoring efforts motivated firms to engage in offshore activities in greater quantities in the 2000s and years after 2010. The argument is that the increase in the prevalence of offshoring outsourcing is attributed to the success of offshoring efforts.

Domestic In-sourcing

Domestic insourcing refers to the activity of contracting out services or goods often manufactured or delivered within the home country borders of the buyer or simply managing services offered internally within an enterprise's home country. Domestic insourcing is central to protectionist debate and discussion of *buy American* (Nordin,& Henrik, 2008). Nordin, and Henrik (2008) believed that domestic insourcing allows businesses to streamline their purchasing and procurement activities, minimize warehouse, transportation and logistics and consequently reduce costs. Nordin, and Henrik further argued that domestic insourcing allows a company to check its local processes and operations, as well as regularly inspect product quality.

Captive Model

Captive model is a *do-it-yourself* approach which refers to the strategic choice by firms to locate organizational activities within their wholly owned subsidiary in a foreign country. This model has been used by multinationals in their overseas deployment. For example, in 2004, multinationals like American Express, British Airways, and General Electric (GE) deployed captive operation model in their overseas subsidiaries. Today, this model accounts for about 60% of the offshore markets. For example, Tesco deployed its substantial internal IT operations in India using the captive approach. The Indian national service companies and software companies-NASSCOM also indicated that 55% of India's offshore businesses assume the captive model.

Re-shoring

The concept of re-shoring refers to the act of reversing the business activities previously off-shored. In the U.S. context, the concept of re-shoring refers to the process of relocating the business operations from the emerging markets or other markets to the United States. As revealed by the Boston Consulting Group survey (Industry Week, 2012), about a third of the U. S. owned manufacturers operating in emerging markets indicated their plan to relocate their business operations back to the United States. Data available on the www.reshorenow.org website also showed that several firms have already re-shored their business operations back to the United States (Reshoring Initiative, 2010).

Joint Venture (JV) Model

The joint venture (JV) model involves parties involved in the business entity creating a legal entity. Each party has a stake in the JV entity and the business activities and objectives of the JV Company are specified in a commercial agreement. Depending on the arrangement, the JV parties may provide management, resource, knowledge, and skilled employees to the entity and share the reward and risk of the venture. This model allows parties to exploit the synergy of mutual objectives and goals for their benefits. Thus, the JV structure can provide an enhanced element of control in an offshore context. The JV structure also allows the outsider to gain access to cheaper resources and specialist knowledge. By contrast, through the JV structure, the local business can gain access to business activity from the outsider.

The cost involved in establishing a JV can be higher than the cost of establishing other models. In addition, a business takes longer to establish a JV than to establish other models. JV also requires parties to dedicate a relatively longer time commitment compared to other models, offering less flexibility to the involved parties. One of the positives of establishing a JV is the ability to result in an organization that can be sold to provide a measurable return on investment (ROI) or one that can be expanded to deliver improved services to other users. Operational issues and the complicated structure often associated with a JV make to be rarely considered by business entities as an optimal offshoring vehicle. However, there are circumstances that limit business entities to the JV structure. For example, in some countries, JVs are required as a matter of policy and to ensure the involvement of domestic businesses in local sectors or markets. JVs can also be selected for offshoring venture for tax reasons. According to Rilla and Squicciarini (2011), JVs tend to work effectively when equal skills are offered to the venture by the involved parties. However, possible conflicts may arise in a JV such as the objective, process, and management clashes, which can lead to failure. The JV approach does not freely provide the user with the right of recourse for non-performance. As such, a JV approach only works if the parties involved in the venture commit to treat a JV as a separate entity.

Hybrid Models

A trend exists in which multinationals seek to ensure that the number of global sources is diversified. In this way, multinationals attempt to avoid the approach of *all eggs in one basket* by going for the hybrid models. This hybrid models are a mixture of offshore and onshore models combined with the thirty party and captive operations. These models are largely favored by software developers.

A hybrid sourcing model makes allows parties to transfer or reverse an offshore operation in cases involving disputed initiative. While a hybrid model may be sometimes easier for parties to manage a single source of supply, it may not be easy to use to achieve the best service. Some multinationals, including Proctor & Gamble and ABN Amro, tend to prefer deploying sourcing offshoring models based on the *best of breed*.

There is also a trend among larger multinational entities to source each service line required from the best vendors especially in cases where a diverse range of services are required by the user. The added advantages of using the hybrid model are the ability to: (a) allow for the movement of enhanced resilience and redundancy of services between providers, and (b) removes a single point of failure. However, it is worth noting that the hybrid model may not be considered the optimal solution. This model requires the parties to pay attention to provider inter-relationships to help prevent finger-pointing between providers and delineate service responsibilities when things go wrong.

The parties must manage and impose the internal governance and the management discipline from the user business. Also, like other offshoring activities, this model requires a clear governance mechanism and escalation routes for managing disputes between the provider and the user.

Application Service Providers (ASP)

The application service providers (ASP) model is geographically neutral, suited to the provision of offshore services. This ASP model involves the provider hosting and supplying services through a remote online connection. The ASP model allows certain service elements to be made available to the world from a central offshore location. However, this model provides limited scope for customization and it is not suitable for all types of services. This service delivery approach has increasingly been favored by Salesforce.com and other multinationals.

Build Operate Transfer (BOT)

The Builder Operate Transfer (BOT) approach encompasses an offshore provider building an offshore service unit that offers its own awareness, knowledge, and skills in the local market. The new service entity is initially owned and controlled by the provider as a group entity. However, after the service unit meets the relevant performance requirements and becomes operational, the control and ownership of the new service is relinquished through an agreed buy-out plan to the user. The BOT model also allows the provider to retain a stake in the business entity and purchase-back the operation. This BOT model is used as a popular solution as an offshoring route by users who lack time, resources, and expertise to create an offshore operation.

The model requires less time than the captive start-up to reach the fully operational status. This model is also a popular offshore route for developing the intellectual property because of allowing the user to control and own the entity used for developing the *crown jewels*. This ownership factor is crucial for venture-backed businesses. In addition, the structuring of the BOT model shields the user business against bearing the associated infrastructure and builds costs. A business entity may also find it difficult to realize the transfer and transition process without measurable and defined operational targets and contractual clarity.

Multi-client Shared Services

Another type of hybrid model is the multi-client shared services approach / model. This one-to-many offshoring model can benefit the larger business, as well as the smaller business. Smaller businesses can leverage resources collected by the provider to serve many parties and thus achieve economies of scale. This model allows a business to access the benefit of investment and a range of resources and scale. The pooled resources and lower costs associated with this model mean: (a) a scalable solution; (b) a commitment-free future and fast implementation; (c) the people; infrastructure and the legacy processes are not inherited by the provider, and (d) greater flexibility for customization.

Multinationals embrace various models of offshoring: domestic in-sourcing, captive model, re-shoring model, JV model; multi-client shared services; BOT model; ASP model; and hybrid model. The choice of one offshoring model over another depends on the objective and goal of offshoring, the benefits associated with the model, as well as prevailing circumstances. For example, multi-client shared services offshoring model can benefit the larger business and the smaller business the model allows a business to access the benefit of investment and a range of resources and scale.

CHAPTER 4. GLOBAL TRENDS IN OFFSHORING OUTSOURCING

The rapid increase in the offshoring outsourcing agreements impacted business by transforming the way they manage their business operations within the globalized world. This trend in offshoring has led to the political backlash, as well as heated debates on the potential benefits and shortcomings of the offshoring. This chapter includes analysis of the trends surrounding offshoring outsourcing phenomenon across the global. The chapter further offers analysis of market trends, location trends of offshoring, operational models used in offshoring outsourcing and prospective of growth.

Global Market Trends

As indicated by Buckley (2011), though outsourcing activities began in the early 1960s when electronic firms started to focus on specializing in the various field, the offshoring activities were largely limited to the oil and gas and energy and utility industry. This trend in offshoring shifted to the manufacturing industry as the dominant sector with highest offshoring activities between 1989 and 2000.

Since 1995, the offshore market expanded rapidly globally. Initially, the offshore market was dominated with IT services largely contributed by the increase in the adoption of computer-related technologies by companies. Initially, firms had trouble in managing offshoring facilities influencing many firms to limit outsourcing production activities to their home countries (Buckley, 2011). However, these difficulties were reduced by the emergency of the Internet and globalization, increasing the possibility to offshore manufacturing activities to Mexico, Taiwan, Singapore, and other selected locations (Buckley, 2011).

After 2000, other sectors that embraced offshoring, included banking and finance, manufacturing, computing and IT, personal and business services, and software services and appliances. According to Buckley (2011), these manufacturing firms initiated outsourcing activities in their home countries before offshoring in other countries. India and China were two countries that benefited from offshoring services. For example, in 1999, India's software exported amounted to US$4 billion and by 2009, the volume of ITO services had grown to US$56 billion (Palugod, 2011). Similarly, BPO services rose from US$12 billion in 2004 to US$38 billion. However, the 2008-2009 financial recession impacted the market for offshoring finance functions but resumed its growth trend in 2010 after the recession. Most of these offshored activities were standardized, knowledge-intensive, and unskilled manufacturing processes with a minimal tariff on reimports (Baily & Bosworth, 2014; Egger, Kreickemeier, & Wrona, 2015).

Emphasizing this view, Egger, Kreickemeier, and Wrona (2015) observed that the growth and technological advancements in information and communication technology (ICT) and globalization was the driving force behind the globalization of service outsourcing and offshoring. These new ICT developments facilitated digitalization, enabling companies to separate service processes. Prior to the ICT revolution, companies had to perform services, including help desks and call centers on site *in situ*. This performing of activities in-house happened because of the expensive nature for companies to set up communication facilities abroad. Among the first simple process offshored services, included help desk operations, data management, computer coding, call centers, and data management. These services constantly evolved and expanded to include services such as benefits administration, financial reporting, and analysis, HR administration, legal services, check processing services, procurement services, and asset management services. These offshored services were later categorized into business process outsourcing (BPO) services and Information Technology Outsourcing (ITO) services (Ottaviano, Peri, & Wright, 2013). These BPO and ITO services evolved to take advantage of arbitrage in cost and skills. However, the outsourcing concept was mainstreamed in the academic literature in the late 1980s.

ITO services included low-end services identified as software maintenance, testing, coding, and higher-end IT related services such as consulting and system integration. Initially, offshoring was limited to low-end services largely because of the shortage of labor for skilled IT specialists in the United States and other developed countries. Typically, ITO involved three services: IT consulting, software services, and infrastructure services. Software services included application development, desktop management, enterprise resource planning (ERP), and application integration. Infrastructure services included network management and applications management. BPO services were classified based on the key business processes involved as customer relationship management (CRM), procurement, finance and accounting, human resource management (HRM), and supply chain management.

This trend in offshoring within the United States is also reflected in a survey conducted by Duke University, Offshoring Research Network. The result of the Offshoring Research Network revealed several trends about the breadth and depth of offshoring (Manning et al., 2008). The survey revealed a forward offshoring trend or a visible shifting trend from the offshoring production facility to offshoring the product development from 2000 through 2008. The trend demonstrates that companies gradually increased the movement of their core competencies to offshore geographical locations since 2000.

The trend also revealed that starting 2000, a significant number of U.S. firms moved from skilled talent capture and low-cost production to offshore value creation, innovation, and acquisition. The R & D expenditures performed abroad by the U.S. parent majority-owned foreign affiliate companies during 1997 and 2008 in India, China, and Brazil. The survey further revealed that there has been an increase in the R & D investments in China by the U.S. companies. This view reinforced by Egger et al. (2015), indicated that since the 1980s, there have been two waves in the manufacturing industry: the offshoring of value-chain activities and the outsourcing of labor-intensive operations, including customer services and IT. This view is also reflected in the other studies (e.g., Egger et al., 2015; Rilla & Squicciarini, 2011) that at present, research and development (R & D) and knowledge-intensive activities constitute the largest portion of value chain activities being offshored by firms.

Offshore Source Market Trends

BPO and ITO continued to be dominated by companies from developed nations from Europe and the United States. For example, in 2008, 60% of India's BPO and ITO exports were contributed by the United States. In terms of offshoring growth rate, the UK market grew by 41% with the rest of other countries in continental Europe growing at more than 50%. On the overall, Europe and the United States are the key sources of offshoring services as they collectively accounted for 79% of India's TCS's revenues in 2009. It is therefore expected that European countries will lead others in adopting outsourcing service models. Countries from Latin (Mexico, Argentina, and Brazil) and countries in Asia (Japan and China) are emerging markets for offshoring (Ottaviano, Peri, & Wright, 2013). According to Ottaviano, Peri, and Wright (2013), telecommunication is the key enabling factor of BPO, sometime referred to as ITES-IT enabled services or ICT-enabled services.

Offshoring Buyer Trends

Larger offshore buyers continue to dominate BPO. Large-sized companies in the global list of best 100, which later expanded to global best 500 companies, pioneered BPO. This trend of dominance by large-sized global companies is expected to be sustained. For example, research shows that from 1996 through 2006, companies with revenues exceeding US$1 billion constituted about 93% of the multi-process BPO. While large players continue to dominate BPO and ITO, mid-market companies are emerging in these spaces. The emergence of mid-market companies and other smaller companies is attributed to several factors. First, delivery models continue to migrate towards third-party service providers facilitating the servicing of a diverse type of clients. Second, providers of BPO delivery matured both in experience and scale increasing the possibility to accommodate smaller companies. Third, the learning curve and common standards of delivery emerged. Last, the learning curve led to the diminishing of the risks associated with outsourcing.

Adoption Trends

In both the BPO an ITO, major adopters of offshoring services are the insurance (BFSI), financial services, and the bank sector. Financial services firms including insurance companies and banks account for the largest percentage of the offshore deals in IT. Other sectors embracing offshoring strategy include manufacturing, high technology, and telecommunication, entertainment, media and entertainment, healthcare, retail, pharmaceuticals, governments, retail, as well as the travel sector. For example, banks are the leading financial firms in outsourcing back office functions including consumer credit, life insurance, payment, and mortgage, IT functions including development, maintenance, and operations, as well as support functions notably property management, procurement, human resources, account receivables, accounts payables, general ledger, treasury, and property management.

Location Trends

China, India, Philippines, and other traditional offshore locations continue to be major offshoring destinations with India dominating others in the ITO class. China, Philippines, and other second-tier countries are expected to become prominent players in the ITO and BPO offshoring. Currently, the

Philippines and India collectively account for the largest proportion of offshored new delivery centers globally.

The number of delivery centers across the globe continues to expand in terms of new locations and scale. The tier 2/3 locations are increasingly becoming dominant arguably because of the large scale, high degree of offshoring maturity, highly skilled talent pool, and low cost. Delivery centers are largely located in the traditional offshore locations' tier 2/3 cities than in the metropolitan areas. Reasons cited for the increasing migration of offshore activities to tier 2/3 locations include infrastructural constraints in metropolitan areas; supply constrains in talent and skills; inflation in Philippines' and India's metropolitan areas; and improvement of local and operating environments in tier 2/3 cities; including social infrastructure, and physical infrastructure (availability, cost, and telecommunications).

Countries such as Philippines, Ireland, Canada, China, and India account for the largest proportion of BPO offshoring market. Other countries including Singapore, Thailand, Vietnam, and Malaysia in Asia, Romania, Ukraine, Czech Republic, Poland, and Hungary in Europe, and Mexico, El Salvador, Brazil, Argentina, Guatemala, and Costa Rica have made inroads in the BPO market.

The global market continues to experience geographical diversifications as a result of the competition among new locations for offshoring. This global diversification trend is partly attributed to competition among destination countries and the adoption of multisource strategies by service providers. Providers and clients appear to be adopting the multisource strategy at an increasing frequency by expanding and diversifying service delivery locations to other emerging countries. This trend seems to be informed by the drive by service providers to leverage on lower cost, skill, and new markets as well as mitigate concentration risk.

Many countries, especially those identified herein, have specific skills and advantages that motivate geographical diversification of offshoring. For example, Thailand is an emerging market for the mature destination with low-cost English-speaking population. Vietnam is an alternative to low-cost destination within a lower cost of IT functions than India and China. Ukraine is emerging as an alternative IT destination with advantages such as technical skills. Turkey has an advantage of language skills that supports German speaking clients while South Africa has skilled personnel in the science and other actuarial areas. Similarly, El Salvador and Guatemala as a potential market for BPO and IT offshoring has the advantage of occupying the same time zone with the United States, Spanish talent, and bi-lingual English, and lies in the same time zone

Trends in Delivery Models

Two delivery models tend to dominate the offshoring market: third-party suppliers and captives. The selection of the delivery model tends to depend on the maturity of suppliers (service providers), the availability, and the type of services. Captives are subsidiaries or divisions of multinational firms in home countries. Captives that serve different divisions of a conglomerate company are called shared services division. Third-party suppliers are vendors of BPO and ITO services. These third-party suppliers can be multinational companies or local companies serving companies located in foreign countries. There are also other non-dominant delivery models in the offshore market namely strategic alliances and joint ventures.

During the initial stages of outsourcing, clients were the primary service providers as owners of subsidiaries in other countries. As primary service providers, clients sought to take advantage of skills and cost differences between countries. As outsourcing evolved, clients were replaced with local third-party suppliers following their acquisition of substantial capabilities. This trend led to the emergence of multinationals in India and China. This trend explains the high number of multinationals from the United States and European countries as reported by World Bank that 16 of 20 top service providers in India are from developed countries, notably the United States and the UK. In India, the dominant IT service providers are third party service providers constituting 75% of the offshore market with captives accounting for the remaining offshore market. However, this pattern is different in other countries that lack local service providers who are sufficiently equipped with capability.

Captive models are reported to dominate these countries' supplier landscape. A typical example is the Philippines with about 90% of captive delivery models dominating the supplier landscape. While captive delivery models seem to dominate the new offshore locations, there appears to be a change in favor of the third-party providers. This change may be explained by the growing trend in the financial services for captive delivery models to divest. This shifting from captives to divest may be motivated by clients seeking to consolidate their finances. On the supply side, the increasing presence of third-party service providers in the global BPO and IT market may have been informed by third party providers acquiring enough financial capability and maturity to take up the operations of captive delivery models.

CHAPTER 5. DRIVERS OF OFFSHORING

Business and Psychological Perspective

In general, the practice of outsourcing has increasingly become a common trend in the global business world. While some researchers approach offshoring from the business perspective, others approach it from the psychology perspective. For example, from the business perspective, Carbone and Moatti (2016) suggested that outsourcing gained wider recognition as one of the best approaches to boost competitiveness and efficiency within the global business world. Carbone and Moatti further opined that the increasing trend in the global outsourcing activities is influenced by the increasing recognition by companies that outsourcing can afford them numerous benefits identified as cost savings; focus on core business; cost restricting; knowledge; contract; access to talent; operational expertise; capacity management; catalyst for change; enhanced capacity for innovation; reduced time to market; commodification; risk management; venture capital; tax benefits; scalability; liability; and creation of leisure time (Carbone & Moatti,

2016; Engardio, 2006). In view of these studies, outsourcing is largely informed by business reasons. For example, according to Engardio (2006), companies opt for outsourcing because they consider outsourcing to be relatively cheaper to contract and subcontracting activities to another company and that this can enable them to gain a competitive advantage achieved through freeing up time, facilities, personnel, and cash. Supporting this view, Norwood et al. (2006) argued that companies choose to outsource their activities to other companies which are deemed as specialists in the determined sphere. Norwood et al. emphasized that outsourcing also enables an organization to receive benefits from pricing and negotiation activities while achieving efficiency in its services. In this chapter, discussions include drivers of offshoring from the business theoretical and empirical perspective, and psychology theoretical and empirical perspective.

Drivers of Offshoring: The Business Perspective

From the business perspective, drivers or motivators of offshoring has been identified from different theoretical perspectives as efficiency (cost reduction); exploitation (developing foreign markets); and exploration (access to talented and knowledge people) (Bierly, Damanpour, & Santoro, 2009; Contractor et al., 2010; Robertson, Lamin, & Livanis, 2010). Cost reduction features in numerous studies as the key driver of global offshoring (Duke University CIBER I Archstone Consulting, 2005; Ellram, Tate, & Billington, 2008; Farrell, 2005). According to Farrell (2005), U.S. companies save $0.58 for every dollar spent on jobs offshored. Similarly, German companies save €0.54 for every euro spend on offshored job (Farrell, 2005). Other drivers of offshoring identified in the extant literature and captured in various business theories, include competitive advantage, location, internalization, and ownership advantages.

Theoretical Perspective to Offshoring Outsourcing Drivers

From the foreign Direct Investment Theory, multinational companies engage in offshoring for direct investment purposes and that the aim is to achieve competitive advantage and absolute advantage. In view of the Direct Investment Theory, companies export products in countries in which there is a comparative advantage over others stemming from labor efficiency (Farrell, 2005).

In the eclectic theory, Dunning (2009) identified internalization, location and ownership advantages as three factors of internationalization that motivate companies to engage in offshoring. In view of eclectic theory, ownership advantages, including economies of scale, brand names, and technology, motivate companies to enter foreign markets as these factors can be transferred between countries. Eclectic theory posits that avoid starting sentence the same way. location advantages possessed by host countries, including lower prices of inputs and abundance of natural resources motivate companies to engage in offshoring activities. The eclectic theory also explains how companies can exploit internalization advantages, including reverse offshoring of services to avoid market imperfection. In this context, reverse offshoring is a form of offshoring which involves firms performing in-house (captive offshoring). Ellram et al. (2008) advanced that firms that undertake their activities in-house are likely to gain ownership advantages, while firms that outsource their services are less likely to gain ownership advantage and thus less likely to embrace internationalization advantage.

For Porter (2008), companies are motivated by competitive advantage to engage in offshoring activities and these advantages are gained through four components: supporting industries, demand conditions, firm structure, strategy and rivalry, and factor conditions. According to Porter, the existence of these four factors serves as motivators for foreign companies seeking to expand their business operations to other countries. Supporting Porter, Doh (2005) held that in case of offshoring, demand conditions for the output of offshoring originate from abroad rather than from the home country. However, in reverse offshoring, demand may come from the home country if the companies perform reverse offshoring in countries which are close to their foreign customers.

The Transaction Cost Theory (TCT), a theory advanced by Williamson also provides insight about re-shoring and offshoring drivers within the emerging market context. The TCT, which features in the strategic management literature, posits that market frictions play a role in transaction costs, uncertainty, opportunistic, and bounded rationality behaviors in the decision made by a firm to restructure its value-chain. Through TCT, Williamson analyses vertical integration and costs and benefits associated with vertical integration to shed light on the role of market frictions on the firm's decision to identify an appropriate entry mode for offshoring core competencies. Williamson further argued that asset specificity, including human, site and physical and commitment (suck costs associated with physical assets) may influence the firm's decision to relocate to other countries. Other studies blended TCT with other theoretical perspectives and used the theory to explain the firm's behaviors in selecting the countries to offshore their business activities (Brouthers, Lance, & Steve, 2008)

Other studies documented in strategic management literature took the approach of a Real Options' theoretical perspective to explain the drivers of offshoring. This Real Options theory is a complementary and alternative perspective to TCT. The emphasis of Real Options Theory is on the competitive advantage as the driver of offshoring and the flexibility of the manager in the company's decision to invest in other countries. In view of Real Options Theory, competitive advantages inform some firms to re-shore (pull back) their existing decisions for core competencies and inform the decision by other firms to make offshoring decisions. According to Trigeorgis (1996), managerial flexibility under uncertainty allows firms to have strategic options when making long-term commitments to engage in offshoring activities.

Relational view (RV) is a variant theory to RBV and TCT. This theory is useful in understanding how competitive advantage can be gained and sustained by a firm. It extends reinforces the view reflected in RBV about achieving competitive advantage. It also serves to compensate for the shortcomings of TCT. According to RBV, a farm to achieve a competitive advantage, it must possess unique resources. These unique resources should be non-substitutable, rare, inimitable, and valuable. From the transaction cost perspective, these unique resources must be specific (Williamson, 1996).

In line with this view, Klein, Crawford, and Alchian (1987) argued that a firm that outsources activities that comprise unique resources, the performance of the firm can be negatively affected by the threat of contract termination and risk of opportunism. Again, from the RV perspective, Mahnke, Lucas, and Vang (2005) advanced that firm can acquire and develop unique resources by establishing and maintaining relationships with external parties: government agencies, customers, and suppliers. Similarly, Dryer and Singh (1998) noted that firms can gain and maintain a competitive advantage by accessing and utilizing in a unique way these critical resources. Taking the RV perspective, Dryer and Singh further argued that competitive advantage is embedded in social relationships arising from the activities outside the firm. According to Dryer and Singh, combined capabilities of parties involved in outsourcing relationship create a relational rent-a supernormal profit. Dryer and Singh further argued that either firm cannot generate relational rent in isolation. Similarly, Haried and Ramamurthy (2009) opined that in an offshore outsourcing relationship, supplier and buyer firms generate supernormal profits by sharing inter-firm relational ties involving mutual commitment and trust from both firms. Relational ties are also reported to provide the offshore outsourcing firm with opportunistic behaviors-safeguards from exchange hazards.

Social exchange theory (SET) also provides insight about re-shoring and offshoring drivers. However, unlike other theories, SET emphasizes behavioral and social aspects of an offshore outsourcing relationship. For SET, the exchange actions occurring between outsourcing firms are contingent on rewarding actions and reactions from other firms. In view of SET, the scarcity of resources initiates social exchange process in an offshore outsourcing relationship, and that resource scarcity motivates parties to engage each other in an attempt to gain valuable input. Thus, SET assumes that exchange firms in the offshore outsourcing relationship seek to gain certain benefits from the process which would not be otherwise achieved if they were alone.

This view means that outsourcing exchange firms are driven by the need to gain certain benefits through cooperation and collaboration. In this case, outsourcing as an exchange process is thought to facilitate an ongoing reciprocal relationship that accrues benefits to the parties involved in the exchange process. It is also argued from the SET perspective that firms in the offshore outsourcing relationship evaluate the benefits of the exchange process based on the benefit and cost analysis. Resources are benefits if they lead to positive outcome whilst resources are seen as costs if they contribute to negative outcomes.

From the RBV of the firm and The Dynamic Capabilities perspective, firms engage in offshoring activities with a view to gain a competitive advantage. In particular, the Dynamic Capabilities Theory posits that the invisible assets of the firm can be used to gain a sustainable competitive advantage. According to Itami and Thomas (1987), the Dynamic Capability Model emphasized the flow of information between the corporate entity and the environment and that indicates that the market and government forces in emerging markets tend to alter the incentive structure with a view to lure companies in developed countries to engage in offshoring activities.

By contrast, from the RBV of the firm perspective, the firm's decision to re-shore and offshore is dependent on the managers' competencies and company resources. In the *Penrose Effect*, Penrose (1959) suggested that the growth potential of a firm is limited to its managers' competencies. Penrose further advanced that company resources and managerial skill set determine the firm's subjective opportunity. Penrose argued that efficiency would suffer if the expansion of the firm takes place at a faster rate than what the management can handle. Penrose held that interaction between the management and resources are the key drivers of change in organizational dynamics. In the same vein, Chandler (1990) held that firms can take advantage economics of scope and scale by increasing their organizational capabilities. According to Chandler, firms must make three inter-related investments in order to increase their organizational capabilities: (a) human resources; (b) global marketing and networking; and (c) production that is proportional to technological requirements. According to Chandler, the three strategies can be achieved through offshoring as one way a firm can use to gain competitive advantage.

An evolutionary theory of economic change advanced by Dosi, Nelson, and Winter (2000), highlighted how a heterogeneous group of firms is driven by the urge for profits to engage in offshoring activities. The evolutionary theory of economic change approach emphasizes that: (a) firms' behaviours reflect strategic orientations and routines traceable to the past and (b) the firms' having decision rules and organizational capabilities that can be modified by deliberate random events and problem-solving tasks. The appealing part of this perspective is the concept of searching for new technology, new markets and organizational structures by firms by embracing offshoring.

Drivers of Outsourcing: Empirical Perspective

Empirically, drivers of offshoring have been identified and categorized as: ownership advantages, location advantages, and externalization advantages. This view is reflected in the OLI paradigm advanced by Dunning (1988) and Lundan (2009). In this paradigm, Dunning suggested that offshore investment is driven by the following factors: location advantages to the host country; firm-specific (ownership) advantages to the foreign investor, and internalization advantages to a foreign country. Doh (2005) agreed with the OLI framework that location-specific advantages one of the determinants behind offshoring. However, Doh questioned internalization advantages and ownership advantages as determinants of offshoring. Similarly, through the Disintegration-Location-Externalization framework, Kedia and Mukherjee (2009) agreed with Dunning that ownership, externalization, and location advantages inform offshoring decisions.

Each of the drivers to offshoring is discussed in the following paragraphs.

Ownership Drivers

Companies engaging in offshoring are required to share their technology and resources including proprietary knowledge, copyright and related rights, patents, trademarks, trade secrets and industrial designs with their subsidiaries. As noted by Wiesmann, Hilletofth, Snoei, and Erikson (2017), the nature of intellectual property, and the laws governing intellectual property varies between businesses, industries and countries. These intellectual property assets and knowledge ownership related factors arguably influence the decision made by companies that engage in offshoring. These ownership drivers are identified into two: technological capabilities and resources and international experience in other countries (Wiesmann et al., 2017).

Technological Capabilities and Resources

Studies suggest that technological capabilities and resources influence firms to engage in offshoring activities (Mudambi, 2008). Mudambi (2008) advanced that organizations with strong technological capabilities and resources are more likely to engage in offshoring activities that organizations with weak technological capabilities and resources. According to Mudambi, firms with more technological capabilities and resources can leverage on these capabilities by outsourcing from external firms. Mudambi further suggested that there was a tendency for resource and knowledge-intensive firms from emerging and advanced markets to disperse their value chain to leverage their capabilities and control costs.

This view is further reinforced by Gottfredson, Puryear, and Phillips (2005) that the innovation process is a complex process encompassing several technological separable stages, and that this complexity makes it difficult for firms to achieve the expected efficiency level across all the stages. Gottfredson et al. believed that this reason informs the decisions made by many firms to outsource some of their activities. On a similar argument, Parmigiani (2007) and others (Afuah, 2001; Rothaermel, Hitt, & Jobe, 2006) opined that some firms embrace the concurrent sourcing strategy when sourcing some activities. The concurrent sourcing strategy involves simultaneously making and purchasing the same services and goods (Afuah, 2001). This argument holds true for technology intensive firms as these firms often focus on searching for efficient ways of organizing and relocating their different services from different countries worldwide. For these firms, the best way to gaining competitive advantage is by outsourcing their best services to the best providers in the world: either because these firms can undertake the task at a relatively lower cost or because they are experts and more specialized. Therefore, it is expected that because of the heterogeneity of resources across different countries, highly resourced firms are more likely than less resourced firms to outsource offshore services.

The argument is that highly resourced firms would need to search for low cost and state-of-the-art providers as these providers can allow outsourcing firms to leverage on their resources and still sustain a competitive advantage over competitors. Mayer and Salomon (2006) support other researchers by arguing that firms that accumulate resources and technological capabilities tend to experience pressure to be better equipped than other firms to enter into outsourcing agreements with foreign firms as well as experience increased pressure to search for the best and world-class suppliers. Mayer and Salomon further advanced that these firms with technological capabilities develop governance capabilities with a view to better select, monitor, and negotiate behavior of suppliers. Firms lacking resources and technological capabilities may also benefit from outsourcing globally; however, such firms may lack the capability to manage outsourcing agreements. Firms lacking enough resources may also face adverse selection problems because of being ill-equipped to identify and select an appropriate external partner and to monitor their performance.

Experience in International Markets

Previous studies revealed that offshore outsourcing decisions may be driven by the ability of firms to search for as well as evaluate external providers (Mol, Tulder, & Beije, 2005; Kogut & Zander, 1993; Rangan, 2000). Rangan (2000) in particular, found that lack of knowledge about external providers influences firms to screen out external sources, and the lack firms' lack of previous interaction with foreign firms increase fear of opportunistic behavior and uncertainty regarding the reliability of external partners. Other studies indicated that firms' international experience is a source of organizational learning (Barkema et al., 1997; Belderbos, 2003; Kogut & Zander, 1993).

Studies also revealed that firms' foreign subsidiaries may motivate firms to engage in offshore outsourcing and that these external subsidiaries may serve as mechanisms for source technology and for accessing local knowledge (Cuervo-Cazurra, 2006; Frost, 2001; Veugelers, 1997). Frost (2001) indicated that firms operating in emerging markets face difficulties in an attempt to identify a capable external supplier from developed countries as well as in managing effectively outsourcing agreements. The argument advanced by Frost is that developed countries tend to have robust institutional environment characterized by political stability and lower levels of corruption. On this basis, firms with previous business experience in emerging markets are reported to be more likely to decide about offshore outsourcing because of the risk and uncertainty associated with the emerging markets (Cuervo-Cazurra, 2006, Veugelers, 1997). In line with this argument, Henisz (2000) argued that policy instability that often characterizes these developing countries may create loopholes domestic service providers to behave opportunistically because foreign firms' restricted capacity to enforce rights.

Location-specific Drivers

As indicated herein, location-specific advantage as identified in the OLI framework is one of the key drivers to firms outsourcing abroad. Foreign Direct Investment (FDI) literature also suggests that overall firms may internationalize their services in an attempt to acquire or explore new technological knowledge for knowledge reasons or for efficient reasons (Hagedoorn, 1993; Hätönen, 2009; Manning et al., 2008; Kuemmerle, 1999; Lewin & Peeters, 2006). In this way, motivations to outsourcing offshore are identified as: efficiency-seeking and capability-seeking. Capacity-seeking relates to the supply agreement between the outsourcing organization and world-class suppliers, whilst efficiency-seeking is in relation to outsourcing agreement between the outsourcing firm and foreign suppliers that have lower labor cost (Cantwell & Santangelo, 1999). On one hand, firms may in seeking to access technological expert, outsource their activities in regions that have technical knowledge and inputs. By contrast, companies located in developed countries may in seeking to minimize costs, opt to outsource their activities to in low-cost countries (Kotabe, 1998; Calderini & Scellato, 2005; Trent & Monczka, 2003). On this basis, one expects that offshore outsourcing decisions by firms may largely be driven by the objective of accessing technological expertise and minimizing labor costs.

Capability-seeking

As suggested by Calderini and Scellato (2005), most of the outsourced services are knowledge-based activities. However, knowledge tends to specific to location as some countries or regions may provide specialized capabilities or know-how within a specific domain. Studies indicated that the dispersion of knowledge-based activities tend to be tied to specific geographical space, suggesting that these activities result from a specialized-niche business activities (Calderini & Scellato,

2005; Cantwell & Santangelo, 1999). Calderini and Scellato argued along with this argument that firms can access this technology expertise and tap these resources by establishing outsourcing agreements with specialized service providers within these regions. In this way, these firms can leverage on the experience of specialized service providers and other benefits. Prior research confirmed that telecommunication infrastructure, cultural similarity, quality and abundance of human capital are location drivers for offshoring (Bunyaratavej e tal., 2007; Graf & Mudambi, 2005; Mudambi, 2008). Mudambi (2008) also found that the majority of engineering activities and other high-end product developments are undertaken in advanced countries. In view of this finding, Mudambi suggested that because world specialized service providers are located in developed regions where knowledge and technology are in abundance, a firm seeking to outsource service will likely outsource offshore to specialized services providers in advanced economies. The argument is that these advanced economies enable the offshoring company to access better centers of excellence or technological infrastructure.

Seeking Lower Labor Costs

As suggested by Kotabe (1998), most offshored activities tend to be knowledge based and labor intensive. For this reason, the cost is an important driver when it comes to firms deciding regarding offshore outsourcing. The argument is that some firms within advanced economies may experience high labor costs than those firms in emerging markets (Kotabe, 1998). Other researchers advanced that some firms outsource their activities in the emerging regions in order to leverage on qualified providers located in low-cost developing countries as this decision provides the possibility of saving on labor costs on the part of the outsourcing firms (Leiblein, Reuer, & Dalsace, 2002; Maskell et al., 2007; Patel & Vega, 1999). These arguments support the proposition that offshoring outsourcing decision by firms may be driven by firms searching for service providers that are more efficient and assure of lower labor costs than those that are less efficient and highly costly.

Externalization Drivers to Offshore Outsourcing

Externalizations drivers, namely technological uncertainty and tacit knowledge are also identified in the literature are drivers of offshore outsourcing decisions (Kedia & Mukherjee, 2009). Kedia and Mukherjee (2009) emphasized that the decision to outsource offshore is dependent on whether it is difficult or easy to externalize a specific transaction. On this account, Kedia and Mukherjee suggested that two service attributes should be taken into account when firms make the decision to offshore outsource: the extent of technological uncertainty of the activity and whether tacit knowledge is a necessity when performing the service. This idea suggests that those externalization drivers and technological uncertainty and the extent of tacit knowledge.

The Degree of Tacit Knowledge

The extent of knowledge tactness being transferred is an important driver to offshore outsourcing for firms that engage in offshore outsourcing (Howell, 1996). According to Howell (1996), the extent of tacit knowledge in an outsourced activity motivate some firms to engage in offshoring outsourcing especially for firms seeking to access technological expertise or specialized know-how. Supporting this view, Williamson (1985) advanced that the odds of a firm getting a specialized external provider will be reduced if the outsourced service is characterized by high tacit knowledge. Williamson further opined that in this case, the firm's propensity to outsource offshore services would be low. Williamson emphasized that the gap in efficiency between the best state-of-the-art supplier and the domestic supplier would be narrow depending on the necessity of the tacit knowledge. Offshore outsourcing will also involve higher coordination costs than those incurred during domestic outsourcing (Kogut & Zander, 1993). According to Kogut and Zander (1993), this happens because it is difficult to codify, articulate, and transfer tacit knowledge, as well as to transfer this knowledge when outsourcing abroad. Kogut and Zander also noted that different cultures of suppliers and clients in different countries make it difficult for tacit knowledge to be transferred.

Technological Uncertainty

Technological change and uncertainty influence firms' decision to outsource or internalize an activity. As argued by Poppo and Zenger (1998), internalizing activities under uncertain technological change imposes inflexibility during outsourcing, and this may influence the firm's decision to outsource the activity to a particular region. Other studies increased use of outsourcing may help a firm respond appropriately to unanticipated market opportunities and threats (Balakrishnan & Wernerfelt, 1986; Hitt, Keats, & DeMarie, 1998;). The argument is that the outsourcing practice may deliver flexibility to the firm.

Balakrishnan and Wernerfelt (1986) advanced this argument by stating that rapid change in technology could render investments in routines and knowledge obsolete because investments in technology are often specialized.

Elsewhere, Kogut and Kulatilaka (1994) opined that during technological uncertainty, firms can engage in international outsourcing with a view to gain flexibility. Kogut and Kulatilaka advanced that flexibility enables firms to switch location when circumstances change as well as adapt to changing circumstances. Kogut and Kulatilaka further noted that the firms' need to access specialized external providers with the necessary capabilities and resources is the key driver of outsourcing decisions involving services characterized by technological uncertainty is the firm. Indeed, Kogut and Kulatilaka demonstrated empirically that technological uncertainty influences the firms' decision to outsource the service to specialized offshore providers.

Elsewhere, drivers of undertaking outsourcing are unique to individual firms' circumstances. The argument is that while some firms engage in outsourcing for competitive advantage reasons, others outsource on other grounds such as gaining core competencies, cost reduction, opportunity to gain relevant specialized knowledge and skills, flexibility from external suppliers, and competitive pressure (Di Gregorio, Musteen, & Thomas, 2009; Dunning, 1998; Farrell, 2005; Gupta & Gupta, 1992; Kakabadse & Kakabadse, 2005; Prahalad & Hamel, 1990).

For Kakabadse and Kakabadse (2005) and others (Di Gregorio, Musteen, & Thomas, 2009), cost reduction is the motivation behind firms engaging in outsourcing. This view is reflected in the suggestion by Dunning (1998) that through outsourcing, firms can exploit cost advantages, including cheaper components, material, and labor, and low transportation costs that often characterized less-developed countries. Farrell (2005) also advanced that firms can utilize savings from outsourcing to re-invest into higher value-added products for customers. For Quinn and Duhamel (2003) and (Prahalad and Hamel (1990), the decision by firms to outsource is largely motivated by the need to gain core competencies. Prahalad and Hamel (1990) argued that firms recognize the value of core competency in sustaining a competitive advantage and recognize that through competitive advantage firms can distinguish themselves from competitors, acquire more customers, and improve their brand loyalty.

In another study, Di Gregorio, Musteen, and Thomas, (2009) revealed that through outsourcing, firms can contract out peripheral activities allowing them to concentrate their investments on activities that facilitate the gaining of competitive advantage. In this way, firms can leverage the supplier's specialized skills and knowledge (Di Gregorio et al., 2009). Costa (2001) reinforced this view by stating that high costs, lack of resources, and lack of the necessary expertise influence firms to contract out peripheral activities to specialized external providers. Others confirmed that through outsourcing, firms can attract and retain highly trained individuals and gain relevant skills and knowledge (Gupta & Gupta, 1992; McFarlan & Nolan, 1995; Quinn, 1999). According to Gupta and Gupta (1992), through outsourcing, firms can acquire specialized knowledge from external providers and avoid risks associated with in-house specialists. Gupta and Gupta further added that by gaining specialized capabilities from external specialists, firms can increase their value and improve their efficiency in serving customers in a cost-effective manner. Quinn and Hilmer (1994) also believed that outsourcing enables firms to access the best global talent and *best-in-world* suppliers. It is also argued that by accessing new technologies and new skills of external suppliers, firms can achieve efficiency and gain competitive advantage (Cavusgil, Yaprak, &Yeoh, 1993). Others argued that by taking advantage of expertise and skills of the best-in-world suppliers, firms become flexible in experimenting new ideas as well as responses to market changes: sophisticated consumers; reduced time-to-market; rapid diffusion of innovation; and intensified global competition (McIvor, 2009; Pinnington & Woolcock, 1995; Tate et al., 2009).

Competitive pressure also features in some studies as a motivation for firms' outsourcing services. McFarlan and Nolan (1995) pointed out that a firm may experience competitive pressure from management attitudes, strong supplier marketing efforts, and external pressure. Tate and Ellram (2009) also argued that through outsourcing, firms can observe and imitate successful industry leaders and lower external competitive pressure.

The Psychology Perspective: Drivers or Motivational Drivers of Task Offshoring

From the psychology perspective, drivers of offshoring, including costs and personal benefits, such as possible loss or gain of attractive jobs / tasks by an organization, may be explained based on various theories in psychology. These theories emphasize outcome expectations as possible motivators or drivers to organizations engaging in offshore activities.

In view of social cognitive theory, outcome expectations are the expected consequences on an individual's behavior. According to Bandura (1997), outcomes that one considers to be attractive motivate behavior that yields these outcomes. For example, onshore members are likely to support offshoring decisions that transfer tasks to an offshore unit if they are convinced that such acts would cause limited harm to jobs or translate into desirable performance outcomes.

Indeed, several studies on offshoring demonstrated that members show a high motivation to take on higher-level responsibilities and tasks with a view to advance in their careers and gain expertise (Demirbag et al., 2012; Mattarelli & Tagliaventi, 2012; Metiu, 2006; Ravishankar, Cohen, & El Sawad, 2010;). Such ambitions are often in high demand and hard to retain at an offshore facility because they create the issue of high turnover of skilled personnel at an offshore unit (Demirbag et al., 2012; Lacity, Iyer, & Rudramuniyaiah, 2008; Lewin & Couto, 2007; Zimmermann, Raab, & Zanotelli, 2012). According to Dibbern, Winkler, and Heinzl (2008), this high attrition rate of skilled employees creates the need for the repeated knowledge transfer and this adds to the offshoring costs, quality deviations, and difficulties in meeting deadlines.

CHAPTER 6.
OUTSOURCING RISKS

Business Perspective: Outsourcing Risks

Many firms operating globally remain concerned about the risk of offshore outsourcing (Ghoshal, 1987). Risks of outsourcing can be approached economics, healthcare, or business perspectives. From the business perspective, outsourcing risks have been identified and categorized differently by different researchers (Barthelemy, 2001; Earl, 1996; Herath & Kishore, 2009; Kotabe & Murray, 2004; Willcocks, Feeny, & Lacity, 2004; Quinn & Hilmer, 1994; Rubin, 2009). For Herath and Kishore (2009), offshore outsourcing risks are reduced product quality, loss of control over suppliers, and undesirable consequences. From the supply chain business perspective, Li and Barnes (2008) identified the risk of offshore at different phases of outsourcing: at phase 1 and phase 2 of the outsourcing process.

Risks at Phase 1 (Ex-ante) Contract Stage

Phase 1 is the ex-ante contract phase. Li and Barnes (2008) noted that risks at ex-ante contract phase occur during contract development, decision-making, and supplier selection stages of the outsourcing process. According to Li and Barnes, during this phase, notable risks are supply market environment risks, namely economic risks, cultural risks, and political risks. Political risks are identified as environmental regulations and laws, unpredictable changes in labor, and political instability (Ellram, Tate, & Billington, 2008; Graf & Mudambi, 2005). Language and cultural barriers are also identified as potential risks to offshore outsourcing (Graf & Mudambi, 2005; Kakumanu & Portanova, 2006; Schniederjans & Zuckweiler, 2004). According to Schniederjans and Zuckweiler (2004), language barriers may lead to conflicts, misunderstanding, and delays by causing communication difficulties between suppliers and the firm.

By contrast, cultural differences such as decision-making styles, social norms, and religion can undermine collaborative efforts during the outsourcing process and hinder the supplier and client firms from establishing trust (Graf & Mudambi, 2005). Economical risks are associated with variability in the currency exchange rate and an inflation rate that impact negatively on the outsourcing firms' financial performance (Dhar & Balakrishnan, 2006). According to Ellram et al. (2008), these macro environmental risks are exceptionally important when making outsourcing consideration and selecting vendors in certain regions.

Risks During the Ex-post Contract Phase

Risks during the ex-post contract phase occur during supplier management stage of the offshore outsourcing process (Lee & Kim, 1999). According to Haried and Ramamurthy (2009), supplier management is an important aspect during the ex-post contract phase of offshore outsourcing yet various risk lies at this stage. Risks at this stage are identified as experience risks; opportunistic behaviors and insufficient capability on the part of the supplier; and unintentional knowledge leakage and conflicts (Costa, 2001). According to Bahili and Rivard (2003), the firm's lack of experience in offshore outsourcing can lead to loss of control over external suppliers, and unexpected management and transaction costs. Studies indicate identify risks of escalating costs linked to unexpected management costs and transactions (Cavusgil, Yaprak, & Yeoh, 1993; Mahnke, Lucas, & Vang, 2005). For Ellram et al. (2008), firms that engage in offshore outsourcing may experience risks related to outsourcing expertise and experience and internal uncertainty in relation to outsourcing requirements. These risks could increase the difficulty for a firm to foresee problems such as hidden costs, management conflicts, and incomplete contract specifications during the outsourcing process (Dhar & Balakrishnan, 2006; Earl, 1996).

Identifying unresolved conflicts as a possible risk during offshore outsourcing, Quinn and Hilmar (1994) indicated that unresolved conflicts during the ex-post contract phase may cause firms to lose connection with their suppliers. Other researchers held that supplier's opportunistic behaviors and lack of capability can lead to quality issues, delayed delivery, and longer lead time periods during offshore outsourcing (Enderwick, 2008; Herath & Kishore, 2009). As described by Aron and Singh (2005), the supplier's opportunistic behavior refers to action taken by the supplier with the view to maximize profits. According to Barthelemy (2003), supplier's opportunistic behavior is caused by the wrong selection choice on the part of the purchasing firm. Barthelemy further noted that this supplier's opportunistic behavior could negatively impact on outsourcing management at this stage of outsourcing. Williamson

(1985) believed that asset specificity is a potential risk during the outsourcing management stage of offshore outsourcing.

In line with this view, McIvor (2009) advanced that managing outsourcing relationships requires firms to make significant relationship-specific investments, such as investments in human and physical assets. In the same vein, Herath and Kishore (2009) noted that asset specificity can cause firms to be in a *lock-in* situation especially where only a few qualified suppliers are available. According to Herath and Kishore, increased transaction costs during outsourcing management may also play a role in increasing the risk of escalating cost.

Other researchers also identify firms' lack of expert and inexperience as the possible risk during the ex-post contract phase, and that these issues may cause conflicts between suppliers and client firms (Mohr & Spekman, 1994; Haried & Ramanurthy, 2009). According to Haried and Ramanurthy (2009), conflicts between the supplier and the client firms during the ex-post contract phase can be triggered by the several factors, namely lack of commitment and trust, unbalanced information, and miscommunication. As argued by Morgan and Hunt (1994), poor conflict resolution at this stage could lead to relationship termination and other destructive outcomes. For other researchers (Aron & Singh, 2005; Kakumanu & Portanova, 2006) an unintended knowledge leak is one of the key risks during offshoring outsourcing. Aron and Singh (2005) clarified that an unintended knowledge risk may occur when suppliers try to steal or misuse proprietary knowledge for other reasons and purposes. Elsewhere, Das and Teng (1996) categorized risks in offshoring outsourcing into two: performance risk and relational risks.

As described by Das and Teng (1996), performance risk arises from a failure to achieve strategic objectives of partners by partners in an offshore outsourcing relationship despite there being cooperation. Performance risk includes factors related to performance that can lead to a reduction in the firm's performance or failure of a partnership. These factors include incomplete contractual specifications and the lack of capability on the part of the supplier. This lack of capability on part of the supplier is reported to lead to reduced quality, delayed delivery, and longer lead time period (Barthelemy, 2003; Herath & Kishore, 2009). Barthelemy (2003) added that the outsourcing firm can make a wrong choice for lacking choices or experience, and this may be caused by lack many suppliers in the market from which to select the specialized suppliers. This could escalate costs and make it difficult for the outsourcing firm to gauge the outsourcing performance (Ellram et al., 2008).

Das and Teng (1996) described relational risk as the consequence of partners in inter-firm partnership fail to fully commit to the joint goal. Das and Teng further opined that the success of supplier-buyer outsourcing relationships depends on the cooperation between the two partners involved. According to Das and Teng, failure of one partner in an outsourcing relationship to cooperate can lead to reduced confidence in the working relationship, and this could lead to increased perceived relational risk. Williamson indicated that outsourcing firms often seek to maximize their own gains and other self-interested benefits. According to Barthelemy (2003), outsourcing exchange firms often display opportunistic behaviors, considered the source of relational risks, identified as secretly misusing a partner's knowledge and skills; unbalanced information, miscommunication, and firms' inexperience. According to Barthelemy, these risks could lead to the termination of relationships and the loss of suppliers by the offshoring firm.

Das and Teng opined that perceived relational risk is related to trust existing between the offshoring firm and the supplier. MacAllister (1995) further reinforced the view by Das and Teng (1996) by identifying two forms of trust in an offshore outsourcing relationship: affect-based trust and cognition-based trust. According to MacAllister, cognition-based trust arises from achievements arising from direct interactions between the contracting firms. Cognition-based trust can also emerge from the knowledge of performance by partners in an offshore outsourcing engagement. For Ring and Van de Ven (1994), cognitive trust is a calculated risk given that the future actions of a partner can be predicted based on the accumulated knowledge of performance in previous deals. On the contrary, affect-based trust as described by MacAllister is established on emotional and social bonds between partners in offshoring outsourcing relationship that extends beyond normal business relationship. In this way, this affect-based trust can affect normal business relationship for partners engaged in offshore outsourcing.

The Psychology Perspective: Offshoring Outsourcing Risks

Various studies that approached offshoring from the psychology perspective suggest that the offshoring experience can be emotionally charged and pose multiple risks to the staff and the concerned company (Morgan & Symon, 2006; Morgan, 2009). According to Morgan (2009), the offshoring decision could make the staff placed at headquarter of the company feel angry, let down, have a feeling of lack of control, and be uncertain about the future. Morgan further added that the staff of the offshoring company may also feel like the company does not value them or understand their experiences.

According to Morgan and Symon (2006), the transferred staffs often remain in contact with the old business entity making it difficult for them to *move-on*" Morgan and Symon further advanced that many individuals affected by outsourcing decision tend to experience the feeling of lack of control. Morgan and Symon argued that for many people, the outsourcing transfer marks the start of other future employment changes. The argument is that outsourcing transfers are often associated with contracts spanning several years and that during these long-term contracts, the employer can make changes at any stage of the negotiation. In the same vein, Morgan (2009) advanced that outsourcing can make the staff to feel that the previous employer treated the badly and be anxious about future changes. Morgan opined that this happens whenever the outsourcing company's changes their work patterns to control costs. These changes could mean deviating from the previous employer's pattern of working.

Studies on downsizing (e.g., Allen et al., 2001) indicated that individuals who retain their jobs during offshoring tend to experience *survivor syndrome*. According to Allen et al. (2001), these individuals tend to experience a mix of guilt and anxiety for being favored by the company and as the next possible victims. Allen et al. further argued that in an outsourcing arrangement, staff retained in the original business entity fits the classic description of *survivor*. According to Allen et al., the transferred staff also fits the survivor description because they survive actual downsizing. The argument is that the transferred staff often experience emotions that are almost like those experienced by staff that lost their jobs. These transferred staff may feel envious of the staff retained in the original company with the consolation that they are not jobless.

It is worth recognizing that there are individual differences in terms of response to situations. While some people may transition with little anxiety, others do not experience strong attachment to the outgoing organization. Still, other individuals may feel attached to their profession and prefer working in an organization that focuses on efficiency and making employees feel valued. Evident suggests that some organizations achieve substantial improvements in outsourcing contracts, and this could create a good working environment for employees. These and other arguments presented herein suggest that outsourcing or offshoring activities are associated with various psychological risks. These psychological risks are largely associated with the ongoing multiple relationships and transfers of employees. Few studies included discussion about these psychological risks yet many psychology theories recognize them to include: exchange theory, identity theory, theories of organizational identification and commitment, and attachment theory.

Stress and Coping

Sverke, Hellgren, and Näswall (2002) recognized that one of the stressors experienced by employees during outsourcing transfers is job insecurity. Sverke, Hellgren, and Näswall advanced that this job insecurity can adversely impact on the people involved in outsourcing transfers. Kinunen et al. (2000) reinforced this view that ongoing situations during outsourcing that do not provide an opportunity to an individual to develop coping mechanisms could be perceived as unfair and lead to ill health. In the same vein, Fineman (2003) argued that people may view outsourcing as an involuntary transition and a threat to their sense of control, and this could make them to lose the sense of belonging and meaning. Fineman holds a similar view that outsourcing may influence people to spend their effort gossiping and politicking an attempt to change an unpredictable into a predictable one. This outcome may lead to emotional contagion and charge. Hallier (2000) holds the view that outsourcing could make the staff to hold security in abeyance as they experience the lack of clarity and uncertainty in the change process. After contract violation by the company, employees could have their view shifted towards a view that their relationship with the company and job is more of a transaction. The result of this change in the perspective may be losing the fundamental reason for work, which could lead to long-term problems. The organizational change may have an emotional aspect, which to a certain extent may be influenced by how people are concerned about changes in their roles and job loss, as well as the extent of their psychological attachment to the organization.

Attachment Theory

Individual need for attachment may influence the relationships between individuals and their organization and colleagues. As suggested by Feeney and Noller (1996) and Bowlby (1969), the construct of exploration is functionally like work and that employees consider attachment function at work as a secure base. According to Feeney and Noller, conditions of chronic and acute stress activate attachment behavior in adults. From this perspective, it can be argued that outsourcing and other major organizational change may influence attachment behavior in individuals. The argument is there are several ways via which outsourcing as a change in the work condition may affect an individual. One of these ways is how others respond to the change in the work situation. Kahn (1998) also believed that people need anchoring relationships while at the workplace (i.e., a secure base). Thus, colleagues can support each other in times of crisis by creating a pace for relational work. For Kahn, the outsourcing process may strengthen or break these relational systems.

Identification

Theories of organizational identification and commitment are used in work psychology to provide an understanding of individual attachment to organizations as related to outsourcing (Klein, Becker, & Meyer, 2009; Van Knippenberg & van Schie, 2000). As indicated by Klein, Becker, and Meyer (2009), in outsourcing, companies often break up groups of people by outsourcing them from different companies. Klein et al. further indicate that the outsourced people may experience disruptions to their workgroup making them upset. Van Knippenberg and van Schie (2000) supported this view by indicating that in professional level outsourcing, employees tend to be remote from their new employer. Sometimes, these new employer moves employees to dedicated offices away from the previous employer. This physical separation of the staff from their previous employer may cause a strain on affective attachment and ultimately lead to detachment. The outsourcing may also impact on an employee's relationships with their new employer (Van Knippenberg & van Schie, 2000).

As reflected in identity theory, some individuals develop pride in an organization or join because of the company's identity. Outsourcing could lead to them being transferred to another organization that they had little information about, they have never heard of, or did not choose to work for the organization. These employees may respond to the telephone is the manner they were used to while working with the original employer, but converse to their previous colleagues from the new employer's perspective. They may feel strange and could lead to difficulties with decision making or problems identifying with the new organization. Studies suggest that perceived organizational identity can impact the out-group and in-group processes, as well as on an individual's sense of self (Albert & Whetton, 1985; Hirschfeld & Field, 2000). As suggested by Hirschfeld and Field (2000), a staff that feels powerless, experience difficult in identifying with the organization, and perceive itself as having little meaning can alienate itself from work.

Exchange Theory

Exchange theory is largely used within the context of work motivation to refer to outsourcing or something else that can be influenced by a change. This exchange theory is crucial in understanding psychological contracts, which synonymous with outsourcing. The theory provides an understanding of how people respond to change. In view of this exchange theory, a psychological contract covers how individuals want other people to treat them and that the psychological contract supplements formal contract between two parties involved in an employment contract (Rousseau, 1995). Studies found a relationship between perceived violation of the psychological contract and reduced performance, trust, citizenship behavior, trust, and commitment (Coyle-Shapiro & Kessler, 2002). This violation of the psychological staff is largely identified as one of the risks of the offshore outsourcing contract. As advanced by Coyle-Shapiro and Kessler (2002), most staff involved in outsourcing tends to feel that the firm that engages in outsourcing transfer often violate their psychological contract. In this way, this contract could potentially create difficult relationships between employees' future and older employers (Coyle-Shapiro & Kessler, 2002). This establishment of short-term limited-security relationships and psychological contract arguably violates employees' need for affiliation and connectedness.

Justice

Fairness or organizational justice is another crucial concept when it comes to outsourcing. There are three forms of justice perceptions as documented in the extant literature: distributive justice, procedural justice, and interactional justice (Byrne & Cropanzano, 2001). Interactional justice focuses on how the interpersonal treatment offered (i.e., respect, dignity, and sensitivity) is perceived as fair or unfair. Procedural justice is based on procedures used, including control of the process, participation, and decision criteria. Distributive justice focuses on the perceptions of fairness, equality or equity of the outcomes. During outsourcing, justice perceptions tend to be negative because managers often impose change based on one-way communication. The uncertainty surrounding offshore outsourcing and managers as employees make them o feel stressed. They respond to mounting pressure to staff whom they assume have been handed over to another organization and thus no longer their responsibility or problem. This way, fair justice is rarely applied during outsourcing and this increases the emotional turmoil and stress on the part of employees.

CHAPTER 7. IMPACT OF OUTSOURCING & OFFSHORING

Long-Term Effects of Outsourcing & Offshoring

Offshoring has been identified with long-term effects, including effects on long-term structural unemployment, wages, productivity, and technology innovation (Tomiura, 2007). Other highlighted long-term effects of offshoring include slippage in environmental and labor standards that apply to products consumed by Americans; decrease in production; and concentration of offshoring tendencies in countries with developed legal and infrastructural base (van Welsum, 2004; Sanchez-Ancochea, 2005). For Whitfield (2017) other long-term effects of offshoring include companies re-adjusting their management practices; offshoring opening multiple opportunities in developed countries and contributing to equal distribution of income and making the globalization processes fair.

Offshoring and Domestic Employment

The potential impact of offshoring on domestic employment is an empirical question that dominates the popular and political discussions at the local as well as international levels. The United States confronted this question when renegotiating the NAFTA with Canada and Mexico. *Tax Cuts and Jobs Act (TCJA)* introduced in 2017 by the U.S. government also considers this empirical question having changed the ways foreign-earned incomes of multinational companies are taxed by the U.S. government. Economics researchers responded to this question with studies that offer varied conclusions regarding the effects of offshoring on domestic employment. While some studies indicated that offshoring drag domestic employment (Egger, Kreickemeier, & Wrona, 2015; Greg, 2014; Gianmarco, Peri, &. Wright, 2013), others suggest that offshoring benefit the domestic labor market (Rosario, 2009; Eli, Bound, & Machin, 1998; Pol, Garicano, & Rossi-Hansberg, 2006). There are also other studies that reported null effects of offshoring on domestic hiring (Robert, 2017; Ann, & McMillan, 2011; David, Jørgensen, Munch, & Xiang, 2014).

Researchers find several difficulties in their attempt to respond to the question of domestic employment that can be affected by offshoring. The first difficulty in understanding the effects of offshoring lies in the conceptualization of the term *offshoring*. For example, some researchers use the term *offshoring* to describe distinct economic activities notably foreign affiliates of multinationals hiring foreign workers (Autor, Dorn, & Hanson, 2013), while others use offshoring to describe the process of multinationals hiring foreign supplies to sell their inputs domestic firms (Hummels et al., 2014). Yet others restrict the use of the offshoring to the process of relocating a domestic plant abroad (Desai, Fritz, Foley, & Hines, 2009). These researchers took different approaches when investigating the effect of offshoring on the domestic labour market (Desai et al., 2009; Hummels et al., 2014; Autor et al., 2013). For example, while Hummels et al. (2014) and Autor et al. (2013) took into account the implications of activities and imports from owned-and-operated and arms-length facilities, Desai, Fritz Foley, and Hines (2009) considered only activities within the foreign companies affiliated to the multinational firms from the United States. These difficulties influenced these researchers to offer different explanation with regard how offshoring may affect domestic employment.

Arguably, these varying forms of offshoring may impact on domestic labor in different ways and require domestic workers to respond in various unique ways that reflect the prevailing economic policies. Consequently, widely different results can be achieved by estimating the effect of these different forms of offshoring on domestic employment. This point is reflected in the evidence by Harrison and McMillan (2011) that domestic hiring by U.S. manufacturing multinational companies does not have similar relationships with offshore hiring activities. Harrison and McMillan (2011) argued that these relationships depend on the activities that occur within the multinational firms' foreign affiliates.

The second difficulty in understanding the effects of offshoring on domestic hiring is the number of channels via which offshoring influences domestic hiring. As argued by Groizard, Ranjan, and Rodriguez-Lopez (2015), a change in the cost of offshoring activity results in offsetting scale effects and substitution effects. While substitution effects lead to a reduction in the demand for hiring at home; offsetting scale increases the demand for domestic hiring. Scale effects lead to a reduction in offshoring costs and cheaper production, which in effect induces firms to expand their level of production. The expansion induces firms to hire more workers abroad and at home (Groizard, Ranjan, & Rodriguez-Lopez, 2015). However, while offshoring firms will hire more workers in response to scale effects, the cost advantages associated with these offshoring activities may induce losses in jobs within domestic industries especially by domestic competitor firms. Researchers often find it difficult to precisely determine the impact of foreign hiring activities on domestic employment because they can only observe one of these margins. Therefore, there is no solid research-based evidence to suggest that offshoring affects domestic employment.

Direct and Indirect Employment Effects

One factor leading to an increased negative public image towards offshoring is the perception that offshoring is accompanied by the creation of jobs abroad. This argument is captured in the following example. The example if one reports that 1000 back-office positions have been offshored by a UK multinational to China, the assumption in the public debate is that net effect of the offshoring choice is the destroying of 1000 jobs in the UK (Görg, 2011). However, this argument may not be true as many parallel indirect and direct effects are put in place making the calculation more complicated than is thought.

It is noteworthy that the relocation of 1000 jobs to China by the UK multination translates to direct displacement of UK employees with Chinese employees. However, the UK multinational's efficiency may be increased as a result of the offshoring of these jobs to China. The argument for the efficiency increases in the UK Multinational's would be that UK employees would specialize in jobs in which they are relatively productive or have a comparative advantage over their Indian workers. The outcome may be the growth of the UK, translating into the creation of new jobs within the UK market in response to the international task specialization based on workers' comparative advantage. In this way, this productivity is attributed to the indirect effect of offshoring.

In view of this example, the productivity and displacement effects of offshoring would be internal to the UK multinational. However, there could be additional effects operating outside the organization's boundaries. The act of offshoring some back-office services to China may directly destroy jobs in the UK for upstream supplies providing those services. Conversely, if the UK's multinational's efficiency is boosted, its customers within the UK market will benefit from more efficient services offered as a relatively lower price. As a result, the business' costs will be reduced and consequently making the multinational more efficient in its operations and possibly fostering its creation of additional jobs domestically through expansion. Analogously for UK consumers, reduced price of services provided by the multinational domestically will enable them to save, and possibly divert expenditure to other domestically supplied goods and services. The impact of this savings will thus be an increase in domestic employment by the UK suppliers.

What the Empirical Evidence Shows

The empirical question is whether job displacement and other negative effects associated with offshoring dominate productivity effects within the offshoring firm's boundaries. A complete answer to these empirical questions needs to consider all these effects; however, the challenge lies in finding data that can meet the completeness requirements. As pointed out by Harrison and McMillan (2011), it is difficult to find data that can be used to measure the effects of offshoring in a cross-country perspective, as well as outside the specific sectors' boundaries. As a consequent, most empirical studies have been restricted to assessing the effects of offshoring within the specific sector and firm that experience offshoring.

Another complication to the question of whether job displacement and other negative effects associated with offshoring dominate productivity effects within the offshoring firm's boundaries is that the domestic loss of jobs by workers is not singularly linked to offshoring, but rather to multiple possible causes. As opined by Harrison, and McMillan (2011), there are multiple other concurrent developments in the labor market known to drive turnover, including competition, customer needs, business context, and technology changes. The effects of these concurrent developments need to be accounted for in studies that associate offshoring with domestic job losses.

Firm-level studies are useful in helping reveal the mechanism via which job losses can occur domestically as a result of offshoring activities (Harrison & McMillan, 2011; Hummels et al., 2011). However, sector-level studies are crucial in quantifying the domestic job losses attributed to offshoring. The challenge for most empirical studies is to reliably measure offshoring effects within the sector. On this basis, there is no empirical evidence to reliably confirm whether job displacement and other negative effects associated with offshoring dominate productivity effects within the offshoring firm's boundaries.

Sector- and Firm-level Empirical Studies

A hallmark study by Hijzen and Swaim (2007) found that a 1% increase in offshoring translates to a 0.08% decrease in services and a 0.15% decrease in sectorial employment. Hijzen and Swaim found that when productivity and displacement effects are disentangled, offshoring does not significantly impact on domestic employment within the same sector. The argument is that jobs created as a result of the productivity effect offsets jobs created as a result of the displacement effect.

In general, evidence from the sectorial studies and firm-level studies suggest that offshoring has a limited impact on sector-level employment (Harrison & McMillan, 2011). However, evidence revealed by Hummels et al. (2011) suggested that variations across workers with different levels of skills with high-skill workers are less likely to suffer, yet more likely to prosper than low-skill workers. Differences are also reported between vertical and horizontal offshoring, vertical offshoring reported to foster domestic employment and horizontal offshoring hurting it (Harrison & McMillan, 2011).

These variations in vertical and horizontal offshoring effects and in skill and occupations among workers motivated researchers to undertake detailed assessments aimed at distinguishing effects of offshoring on workers occupations and skills. The argument is that the impact of offshoring is complicated by the sectorial perspective as offshoring largely focuses on sectors impacted by offshoring rather than focus on other sectors that have workers employed with similar skills and occupations (Ebenstein et al., 2014). This action of neglecting other sectors causes studies to erroneously stress the weighted average exposure of occupation offshoring across sectors. In this form of exposure to offshoring, each exposure of the sector is weighted based on the proportion of workers within the occupation (Ebenstein et al., 2014). This method of measuring occupation exposure based of the link between data on individual workers and sector-level data on offshoring demonstrates a divergence between the impact of occupational exposure and sectorial exposure on wage outcomes.

Negative effects of offshoring on workers' wages are sizable when exposure to offshoring is at the occupational level but not at the sectorial level. The idea is that occupational exposure exerts downward pressure on workers' wages by relocating domestic workers between lower-wage manufacturing jobs and higher-wage jobs in other occupations and sectors. When the impacts of offshoring across different sectors are considered, this downward pressure is reinforced depending on the form of workers' occupation. However, the negative impact of offshoring on workers' wages may be shielded by the interactive and non-routine job tasks (Baumgarten, Geishecker, & Görg, 2013). The highly educated workers are favoured when occupational exposure exerts downward pressure on workers' wages causing a shift towards more interactive and non-routine tasks (Baumgarten et al., 2013). For example, offshoring within multinational service providers and manufacturers has been found to lead to the upgrading of skills for domestic jobs.

As revealed by Becker, Ekholm, and Muendler (2013), this shifting from non-interactive and routine tasks towards interactive and non-routine tasks indicates that interactivity and non-routineness are inversely related to offshoring. This inverse relationship between interactivity and non-routineness and offshoring has influenced researchers to investigate the interactions between workers' skills and tasks' routineness (Acemoglu

& Autor, 2011). According to Acemoglu and Autor (2011), tasks routineness facilitates automation, and automation could replace workers with substitutable skills at the domestic level without the effects of offshoring. Examples of jobs that are characterized by routine include manual and middle-skilled cognitive jobs, such as clerical work, monitoring, repetitive production, and book-keeping. These tasks are defined by one feature: accomplished according to practices which can be codified and follow well-understood, defined and precise procedures. In this way, these routine tasks can easily be implemented by foreign workers remotely or by machines when translated into mechanical instructions.

In line with this view, Costinot and Vogel (2010) pointed out this process of computerizing routine tasks facilitated the hallowing out of administrative and clerical occupations the U.S. and other high-income countries. According to Costinot and Vogel, routine tasks can be codified in computer software and this makes it possible for workers or machines abroad to perform them. This has been wrongly construed to suggest that computerization has made routine tasks less important. This computerization of routine tasks simply means that companies are increasingly reallocating tasks that require workers to devote their time to gathering, analyzing, organizing, and transmitting information to offshore workers and machines. The argument is that technological advances progressively reduces the cost of offshoring these information-intensive tasks. Acemoglu and Autor (2011) demonstrated that the offshoring and automation of routine tasks positively impacts on demand of workers with the skills that are necessary to undertake complementary non-routine tasks. Acemoglu and Autor further partitioned non-routine jobs into two categories: abstract tasks non-routine tasks, and manual non-routine tasks. Non-routine tasks include tasks that involve intensive problem-solving activities. These non-routine tasks also require creativity, persuasion, intuition, and high levels of analytical skills and education, and characterize creative, technical, managerial, and professional occupations, including those in science, medicine, design, management, and engineering. Non-routine tasks are intense in problem-solving, analytical reasoning, and creative thinking making them complementary to computerization and automation. These intensive problem-solving activities jobs also rely heavily on technological advances that minimize the cost of collecting, analyzing and systematizing information as well as on information content. This reliance on technological advances and information content makes these tasks to increase the demand for workers with the ability to perform abstract tasks. These jobs are in high demand, yet the workers with the ability to perform them are scarce especially in developing countries. Consequently, companies are less likely to offshore these tasks from lower-income countries.

On the other hand, non-routine manual tasks encompass activities involving visual and language recognition, situational adaptability, and person interactions. These tasks may not require formal education beyond the high-school level; however, they are often performed in person in specific places where services are offered. This makes it impossible to offshore non-routine manual tasks. These tasks include mundane activities that require physical workers. Typical examples of these tasks include cleaning an office, cooking a meal, installing a wooden floor, and driving a bus. These tasks, especially service tasks such as janitorial and cleaning work, food preparation and serving, in-person health assistance, ground cleaning, and maintenance, do not usually require formal education beyond high-school level (Acemoglu & Autor, 2011). These tasks cannot be automated because they require freedom to respond to environmental and work interactions, as well as environmental and interpersonal adaptability, which cannot be captured in the computerized set of procedures.

Therefore, it is important for researchers, companies, and individuals seeking to understand the offshoring effects to understand the interactions between workers' skills and routines of tasks. The argument is that companies can use offshoring and automation to cut into domestic worker's employment by replacing those with skills involving interactive and non-routine jobs. By contrast, offshoring and automation may facilitate the employment of domestic workers with skills involving interactive and non-routine jobs so long as these workers complement the system. These differences suffice as explanations to the employment polarization that characterize developed countries where the occupational tasks are offshored (Acemoglu & Autor, 2011).

The Devil Is in the Details

An in-depth analysis at the individual firm-level reveals that a small aggregate net impact of offshoring activities on domestic employment may mask a significantly bigger change at a disaggregated level regarding the distribution of losses and gains among domestic workers with varying skills. Recognizing that not all jobs require workers to have same skill content, one can gain additional insight by analyzing the impact of offshoring on matching of workers' skills and task skill requirements (Costinot & Vogel, 2010).

In principle, relatively different workers' skill abundance and tasks skill intensities in high-income countries may offer a comparative advantage to workers with high skills in complexity tasks. As a consequence, other individuals with high skills in complex tasks may be attracted to high-income countries leading to a high number of such workers in high-income countries. The effect of this advantage to workers with high skills in complexity tasks is complex jobs staying while the less complex jobs getting offshored. In this way, easier offshoring causes task upgrading by pushing domestic workers to take on more complex jobs. The consequence of this effect of offshoring is an increase in domestic employment and wage inequality among workers with varying skill levels as a result of increased supply of low-skill cheaper labor.

These predictions are however, difficult to confirm because they require one to have detailed information on workers' skills, as well as the complexity and nature of tasks undertaken by offshore and domestic workers. While useful information on domestic workers is provided by the United States and Germany, no such information is provided on offshored workers. This makes it difficult for one to precisely determine the attributes of offshore workers and tasks (Hijzen, & Swaim, 2007).

Kovak, Oldenski, and Sly, (2017) addressed the simultaneity between offshore employment and domestic employment by exploring the decline in cost of offshoring exogenous to choices made by a firm. Kovak et al. specifically analyzed the changes in the cost of offshoring associated with bilateral tax treaties (BTTs) that allow U.S. multinationals to avoid double-taxation. BTTS, as described by Kovak et al., reduces the constrain of double-taxation by lowering the effective tax rate imposed on incomes generated from foreign subsidiaries ultimately bringing down the offshoring associated costs. This study leveraged the double taxation incidence across industries, the country mix of multinational affiliates, and differences in the timing of treaties to suggest that BTT induce changes in U.S. domestic employment and in foreign affiliate employment.

The Kovak et al. (2017) study further investigated the effects of offshoring hiring on domestic employment by examining the impact of offshoring on employment using U.S. multinational firms. Result revealed that within multinationals a decline in offshoring cost induces a positive effect on domestic employment and these effects outweigh the negative effects of substituting domestic employment with employment abroad. An increase in employment in U.S. multinationals' foreign affiliates causes an economically modest and statistically significantly positive impact on the employment at home (Kovak et al., 2017). Specifically, the result showed that a 10% increase in employment in the affiliate firm induced by BTT translates to a 1.9% increase the U.S. parent firm's employment (Kovak et al., 2017).

This BTT-induced positive effect of offshore employment suggests the positive effects associated with lower offshoring costs in foreign countries where affiliates are established outweigh the substitution effects but masks substantial heterogeneity in U.S. parent firms. The idea is that U.S. multinational companies that establish a new foreign affiliate after entering a new BTT do not cause a change in domestic employment. Kovak et al. (2017) further assessed the impact of changes induced by BTT in offshore hiring on domestic employment induced by industry changes (Kovak et al., 2017). In this way, the study hypothesized that U.S. multinationals could respond to industry-wide alterations in offshoring costs by adopting foreign suppliers at the expense of the domestic one, and that lower costs realized by multinational firms could pose a competitive pressure on domestic firms. The findings showed that offshoring activity by multinationals have industry-wide affects; however, these effects largely depend on the nature and type of offshoring activity (Kovak et al., 2017).

In view of this study findings, negative and positive effects of offshoring by multinationals offset each other because the study did no find offshoring to cause a discernible effect on industry-wide domestic employment (Kovak et al., 2017). However, among the vertically oriented multinationals (i.e., multinationals that obtain sales from affiliates in foreign countries), BTT-induced increase in offshore employment generates a statistically significant decline in industry-level hiring. Based on this study's estimates, among vertically oriented multinationals, a 10% BTT-induced increase in employment in multinational firm subsidiary translates to a 0.4% decline in industry employment. This different outcome for different types of multinational firms suggests that the offshore effects are dependent on the activities of the multinational.

The argument is that multinationals that focus on sourcing inputs from other countries are more likely to prefer substituting between abroad and at home than those that focus on opening foreign affiliates. Overall, this study revealed that offshoring affects employment level in foreign affiliates' countries at both the industry level and firm level (Kovak et al., 2017). These findings also showed that a decline in employment in some multinational firms' parent country is offset by an increase in employment at the foreign affiliates' country, and this yields a positive net offshoring effects on domestic employment though with substantial reallocation and dislocation of workers.

Studies also revealed that high-skilled jobs in Europe gain from offshoring (Harrison & McMillan, 2010; Neureiter & Nunnenkamp, 2010; Paul & Yasar, 2009). These findings are further confirmed by Simpson (2012a) using UK firms. In this study, Simpson (2012a) revealed that offshoring facilitates the relocation of low-skill activities to emerging low-wage countries, and that this move positively impacts on complementary high-skill activities in the home country. Simpson (2012b) revealed a similar effect for firms operating in low-skill industries. Becker, Ekholm, and Muendler (2013) replicated these findings using German multinational firms. Becker et al. found an association between offshoring and a shift towards more interactive and non-routine tasks in jobs characteristics in German multinational firms. Based on the results of these studies, offshoring affects employment level in foreign affiliates' countries at both the industry level and firm level.

On the empirical ground, other scholars seem to agree that an increase in employment in developed countries such as the UK and the United States in favor of high-skilled workers is an outcome of an outward transfer of skilled demand (Acemoglu, Gancia, & Zilibotti, 2012; Autoret al., 2013; Autor et al., 2008). Many studies highlighted the determinants of this shift in skilled labor demand skill biased technological changes (SBTs) (Acemoglu et al., 2012; Autor, Katz, & Kearney, 2008).

Other influential studies suggest that what influences the domestic labor market is trade in material and input offshoring, among others (Federico, 2014; Görg, 2011). Görg (2011), one of these influential studies on the negative relationship between domestic employment and trade, provides a summary of a discussion on effects of offshoring and globalization on employment in advanced industrialized countries and concludes that offshoring may cause high job turnover in developed countries in the short run. However, Görg argued that there is no sign that offshoring or trade causes lower employment or higher unemployment overall in the long run, even though it may have a slight impact on the employment of low-skilled workers. Therefore, results are mixed in regard to whether offshoring or trade causes lower employment or higher unemployment overall in the long run. On this basis, it is unclear whether offshoring or trade causes lower employment or higher unemployment overall in the long run.

CHAPTER 8.
IMPACT OF OFFSHORING AND PRODUCTIVITY

Productivity Gains

Self-selection bias increases the difficulty for researchers to measure productivity gains from offshoring. Despite this self-selection bias, several empirical studies found evidence that firms engaging in offshoring tend to achieve productivity benefits. However, the findings of these studies differ by country (Amiti & Konnings, 2007; Halpern, Koren, & Szeidl, 2015; Topalova & Khandelwal, 2011).

Offshoring and Productivity

Within the Indonesia context, Amiti and Konnings (2007) used manufacturing plant-level census data for the period 1991-2001 to estimate the gains in productivity from reducing trade tariffs on intermediate inputs and final goods. The study findings confirmed that lower output tariffs can induce tougher import competition and lead to an increase in productivity.

Similarly, cheaper imported inputs may increase productivity through quality, variety, and learning effects. In particular, the finding showed that a 10% decline in input tariff translates into a 12% productivity gains for firms that engage in importing their inputs, and that productivity gains achieved from reducing input tariffs are about two times as high as productivity gains from lowering output tariffs (Amiti & Konnings, 2007).

In a similar study, Kasahara and Rodriguez (2008) used plant-level data obtained from the Chilean manufacturing firms for the period of 1979-1986 to examine the impact of intermediate goods importation of plant productivity. Results confirmed that importing foreign intermediates significantly impacts firm productivity. The study found evidence across different estimators that importing foreign intermediates significantly improve the productivity of the plant (Kasahara & Rodriguez, 2008).

Halpern, Koren, and Szeidl (2015) replicated the findings by Kasahara and Rodriguez (2008) within the Hungarian context. In this study, Halpern et al. used plant-level data obtained from Hungarian firms to investigate a variety and a quality channel via which imports (imported inputs) can impact on the productivity of the firm. Results suggested that the importation of inputs increase the productivity of the firm by 14% with two-thirds of this productivity linked to the increase in the intermediates variety used in production. Results also showed that the importation of all input varieties increases the revenue productivity of the firm by 22%, with one-half of this productivity attributed to imperfection substitution between domestic and foreign inputs (Halpern et al., 2015). The one-quarter of productivity gains by Hungarian firms was attributed to imported inputs.

Boler, Moxnes, and Moe (2015) further reinforced these findings. Boler et al. studied the join complementarity of imported inputs (intermediates) and R & D cost shock on firm productivity and performance, and the impact of R & D cost shock on imported inputs and R & D investment in Norway. Imported inputs was introduced into an endogenous productivity and a model of R & D and demonstrated that international sourcing and R & D are complementary activities. Results also revealed that with the exogenous tax policy, cheaper R & D stimulates the imports of intermediates and R & D investments quantitatively.

Moser and Zurich (2010) used a difference-in-differences matching approach and a sample of German establishments to examine channels via which offshoring impacts on domestic employment. The study identified offshoring establishments based on the increase in the volume of foreign inputs to total inputs and found that offshoring establishments report higher foreign and domestic market share, higher productivity and higher employment than if they did not practice offshoring. In addition, the production depth of offshoring establishments remains unchanged suggesting that offshoring largely operates by substituting domestic suppliers for foreign suppliers, rather than operating by reducing home production.

The Moser and Zurich (2010) study exploited the differences between offshoring firms that do not restructure parts of their establishment and those that structure parts of their establishments, and further identified a positive productivity effect of offshoring on employment. In particular, the study found an economically and statistically significant positive effect of offshoring on employment and statistically significant effect of an increase in input share (offshoring) of foreign intermediate on the domestic firm (Moser & Zurich, 2010). The study also found that on average offshoring does not significantly affect production depth, and does not replace a production by foreign supply, rather substitutes domestic suppliers for foreign suppliers (Moser & Zurich, 2010). Thus, in this study, Moser and Zurich found that offshoring firms improve their competitiveness by increasing their average labor productivity, as well as increase their foreign and domestic market share against plants that do not engage in offshoring.

The Moser and Zurich (2010) study constructed three important treatment variables at the firm-level that facilitated the identification of productivity and downsizing effects of offshoring on domestic employment. The first treatment variable is the defining offshoring (i.e., as offshoring-sine-restructuring) in a manner that does not overlap with any simultaneous restructuring such as spin-off, sell-off, or partial shut-down. The second treatment variable is offshoring-cum-restructuring, which is offshoring accompanied by simultaneous restructuring event. The third treatment variable is the foreign-supplier-switching, which entails switching between non-European Union and European Union suppliers (Moser & Zurich, 2010).

Schwörer (2013) analyzed descriptively domestic outsourcing and offshoring practice in nine countries in Europe between 1995 and 2008 and concluded that productivity gains in established firms was largely driven by gains of multinational enterprises. Foster-McGregor, Stehrer, and Vries (2013) adopted estimate translog cost function and a standard approach to assess the effect of offshoring on cost-shares of domestic workers with varied skills. Based on the result of this study, the largest impacts of offshoring were observed for workers with medium skills. Similarly, Parteka and Wolszczak-Derlacz (2015) assessed the effects of offshoring on wage convergence and wage growth in manufacturing sectors using data obtains from 27 countries in Europe. Results reported by Parteka and Wolszczak-Derlacz showed that even though offshoring causes a reduction in the wages of less-skilled workers, the extent or magnitude of these effects is economically negligible. Worth noting is that Foster-McGregor et al. employed a set of sectors and countries used in the study by Parteka and Wolszczak-Derlacz suggesting that these studies complement each other.

Ghosh (2017) used firm-level microdata from Spain's manufacturing sector to study the effect of offshoring on the labor market outcome and firm-level productivity (i.e., total factor productivity (TFP) during the 2008 financial period. In this study, Ghosh (2017) analyzed the impact of offshoring on firm-level productivity in a two-step process. The first step revealed that offshoring leads to increases in R & D and higher R & D expenditures when other industry and firm specific non-trade and trade channels are controlled. In this step, Ghosh provided robust evidence suggesting that offshoring impacts on the overall employment by fostering within-firm reorganization reflected in skill composition, and that this reorganization is driven by an increase in the number of regular non-skilled workers. This increase in non-skilled workers offsets the weak negative effects of offshoring on temporary employment.

In the second step, Ghosh (2017) demonstrated that offshoring directly affects the firm's productivity via several channels. The first channel is that offshoring incentivizes the firm to be engaged in productivity-enhancing investments such as expenditure in R & D, as well as reduce marginal costs. In this sense, the firm raises profits and minimizes marginal production costs by sourcing cheaper intermediates, and this allows it to boost productivity by profitably undertaking R&D expenditure. The intuition is that cheaper intermediates resulting from incentive structure and trade liberalization lead to increased profits and productivity, and other gains notably the declining trade barriers and a fixed R & D cost on the firm's future value. Gosh further demonstrated that offshoring leads to reallocation of resources within the firm by inducing a decline in the number of temporary lower end of skill workers who undertake routine jobs. In contrary, offshoring was found to significantly and positively affect within firm level skill composition by inducing the hiring of R & D workers. This suffices as the explanation for firms' decision to offshore low-skilled jobs to countries known for low wages and hire skilled workers with the aim of boosting their productivity. The Ghosh study also demonstrated that firms undertaking R & D and imports are more productive, larger in size with a significantly high likelihood of survival.

In another study, Amiti and Wei (2006) indicated that in the United States, service inputs offshoring accounts for a larger proportion of productivity gains from manufacturing than offshoring of material inputs. The U.S. offshoring firms are outstanding in productivity growth and in other regards prior to offshoring yet these firms continued to experience growth in productivity gains even after the onset of the offshoring activities (Kurz, 2006). On the contrary, in Canada multifactor productivity gains significantly contributed by material offshoring with no evidence of service offshoring (Baldwin & Gu, 2008). Olsen (2006) also provided further evidence of a causal link between gains in productivity and offshoring.

Other researchers suggested that technology play a significant role in the rise of offshoring activities and productivity gains from offshoring. For example, Bloom, Sadun, and Van Reenen (2005) demonstrated that affiliates of U.S. owned multinational firms within the UK make better use of technology than subsidiaries of multinational firms owned by other countries. Bloom et al. further advanced that this more effective utilization of technology by affiliates of U.S. based multinational firms lead to greater growth in productivity from offshoring than those achieved by affiliates of multinational of other countries. Software standardization and technological improvements also played a role in enhancing productivity growth from offshoring activities. The argument is that technological improvements and software standardization allows multinational firms to purchase services based on software standardization and advanced technologies without incurring sunk costs (Bartel, Lach, & Sicherman, 2005). Grossman and Rossi-Hansberg (2006) advanced a similar argument that a drop in the price of ICT technologies that facilitate offshoring may induce firms to invest more in these ICTs, and this may translate into the productivity of workers who make use of these technologies.

Trade theory posits that offshoring activities may increase the firms' productivity by generating gains for low-skill workers at home through intensively using these workers (Deardorff, 2001). In view of this theory, it is easy to move offshore certain forms of production tasks or activities, and that firms that use these activities or tasks intensively should reap large productivity gains achieved by offshoring more workers. However, the trade theory also posits that the offshoring is likely to lead to the displacement of some of these workers, and that these workers will be required to "re-tool" and adjust to the changing circumstances. Rossi-Hansberg (2008) reinforced this view in their seminal paper that offshoring may lead to a reduction or increase in the equilibrium wage of domestic workers with low skills, and that the effect of offshoring on equilibrium wage of domestic workers with low skills depends on the size of country within the global markets, extent of displacement of domestic workers, and sizes of productivity growth.

A similar study by Schworer (2013) considered the differences between supplier changes, domestic outsourcing, and offshoring while investigating the trend in offshoring activities in Europe between 1995 and 2008. The study findings revealed that manufacturing activities were systematically offshored, whereas service activities were systematically outsourced and offshored during this period (Schworer, 2013). The study found that a firm's overall share of internal production reduced by 4.5% points (Schworer, 2013). However, the combined firm panel data and industry-level data on domestic outsourcing and offshoring contributed to gains in productivity. These productivity gains were linked to gains recorded by multinational enterprises suggesting that offshoring leads to productivity gains.

In a separate study, Görg and Hanley (2011) showed that material offshoring led to the gain in productivity, especially among Irish electronic exporters with low export intensity. Similarly, Egger and Egger (2003) empirically demonstrated that offshoring enhances the productivity of low-skilled workers in the long run but decreases their productivity in the short run. In another study, Görg, Hanley, and Strobl (2008) reported that service offshoring raises the productivity of exporting Irish manufacturing firms. Hijzen, Inui, and Todo (2008) replicated these findings.

In this study, Hijzen, Inui, and Todo (2008) found that Japanese manufacturing firms that offshore their activities to foreign firms raise their productivity; however, no such effect was found for firms that offshored to external suppliers. Similarly, Amiti and Wei (2009) noted that offshoring enhances productivity by indicating that material offshoring material and service offshoring in the United States accounted for 10% and 5% of the productivity growth among the U.S. multinational firms. Similarly, Milberg and Winkler (2010) found service offshoring to enhance the productivity of German manufacturing firms when domestic outsourcing was controlled. In view of the results of these studies, offshoring leads to productivity gains.

For Olsen (2006), offshoring is thought to enhance productivity in various ways. First, arguments include that offshoring allows firms to specialize by reducing the scope of work that are undertaken in-house. In this way, offshoring some tasks can allow firms to focus on core activities or functions. Second, it is argued that offshoring allows the firms to free up resources by offshoring low-cost inputs and invest these inputs in productivity-enhancing technology and capital. Third, offshoring is believed to facilitate firms to change the composition of their labor force and adopt new and productive enhancing practices (Baldwin & Gu, 2008). The argument is that offshoring is a business restructuring strategy that allows firms to restructure their labor force. Last, offshoring allows firms to offshore some tasks to firms more technological advanced and this this strategy may allow final producers of goods to learn from foreign suppliers the process of productivity-enhancing production (Amiti & Wei, 2006).

In a similar study Michel, and Rycx (2014) used industry-level data for Belgium for the period 1995–2004 to empirically examine the impact of business and materials services offshoring on productivity. Results showed that business services offshoring in manufacturing leads to productivity growth; however, material offshoring causes no productivity effect. The results further demonstrated offshoring causes rent spill overs suggesting that productivity gains due to offshoring in one industry may be affect other industries especially those that purchase the output of the industry involved in offshoring. However, this outcome happens only if the value to the user surpasses the output price.

Conclusion

In view of the findings of the studies reviewed herein, offshoring can enhance productivity in several ways. First, offshoring may accompany restructuring measures which minimize inefficiencies. For example, offshoring may influence the firm to improve the reporting and communication system between departments or how tasks are bundled. Second, offshoring may lead to a static efficiency gain. This outcome may occur when offshoring firms focus on core competencies. Third, offshoring facilitates interactions between internal and foreign suppliers allows firms to benefit from learning externalities. For example, the offshoring firm's workers may gain knowledge about technologies and other innovations from foreign suppliers or learn about other software packages adopted by foreign suppliers.

Offshoring may also increase the productivity of the firm especially when the input varieties imported by the firm better match with the firm's specific needs or as of higher quality. Fifth, offshoring to developing and low-wage countries may raise profits and lower the marginal production costs thus creating resources for investing in R & D. In this way, offshoring may enhance productivity by increasing innovation. Görg and Hanley (2011) empirically confirmed this hypothesis using data from Irish Plant-level data. Last, offshoring may induce selection effects and tougher competition in the markets as well as general equilibrium effects especially if productivity gained from offshoring spill over to other firms. Accordingly, offshoring leads to productivity gains for firms that engage in offshore practices.

CHAPTER 9. LABOR MARKET EFFECTS OF OFFSHORING

Offshoring and Labor Market

Over the past several decades, firms in developed countries have been engaging in offshoring, either by internationally outsourcing through purchasing intermediate inputs from foreign suppliers or relocating their low-skilled labor intensive production services through vertical Foreign Direct Investment (FDI) to foreign affiliates. In theory, offshoring may negatively or positively affect the firm's environment. Positive labor market effects may emerge as a result of offshoring if cost savings facilitates firms to increase their market share globally and competitiveness; negative labor market effects could arise from the relocation of production abroad and downsizing. The empirical question to ask is which channel dominates another.

Several studies empirically investigated the relationship between offshoring activities and home country (domestic labor market). While findings of empirical studies on macro-data demonstrated small or insignificant negative labor effects of offshoring; empirical studies using micro-data reported mixed findings (Freeman, 2005; Moreno-Brid, & Santamaria, 2005). While some micro-data studies reported negative labor effects as a result of offshoring, others reported positive labor market effects (Kohler, 2004; Razzolini & Vannoni, 2011). These contradictory findings failed to disentangle different channels via which offshoring impacts on domestic employment either negatively or positively.

As estimated by OECD (2013), about 70% of services imports globally are intermediate services with 50% of the manufacturing imports globally as intermediate goods (semi-finished products, parts and components, and primary goods). In view of these statistics, researchers cannot ignore the potential effects of cross-border production disintegration. Similarly, many labor markets in emerging markets such as? continue to experience rapid labor demand changes and/or changes in wage structure (an increase in wage inequality and a decline in demand for less-skilled workers) (Acemoglu & Autor, 2011; Feenstra, 2010). These tendencies generated a common fear widely expressed by policy makers and employees mainly from industrialized countries. The fear emanates from the notion that offshoring and trade opening to low wage developing countries may adversely affect wages and employment in the offshored countries. These threats of possible negative effect of offshoring, especially in terms of lowering wages and cross-border labor substitution of low-skilled workers at country that offshores the services, have increasingly become a critical theme in applied-policy research debates, as well as a general policy issue (Bottini, Ernst, & Luebker, 2011; Milberg & Winkler, 2011; World Trade Organization [WTO], 2007, 2011).

Political debates have been dominated with these worries regarding possible implications of trade integration between developing and less developed countries. Studies (e.g., Feenstra & Jensen, 2012; Parteka & Wolszczak-Derlacz, 2015) exacerbated these worries by suggesting that about 40% of U.S. manufacturing jobs have been offshored to low-wage countries. These debates informed forced researchers to pay attention to the effects of offshoring on the labor market and employment (Feenstra, & Jensen, 2012; Wolszczak-Derlacz & Parteka, 2015). For example, Wolszczak-Derlacz and Parteka (2015) focused on offshoring and employment trends observable in countries in Europe with a focus on the offshoring-employment relationship. In this study, Wolszczak-Derlacz and Parteka analyzed data covering a wide European panel encompassing 27 European Union (EU) countries and involving 13 manufacturing sectors for the period 1995-2009 by assessing the sector-level intensity of offshoring decomposed into foreign and domestic components. Results of the panel data model estimation suggested that increased offshoring pushed down the domestic employment in the EU manufacturing sector. More specifically, results revealed that workers most affected by offshoring were low-skill workers, pinned to the shrinking labor demand at the country where multinationals are based (i.e., the home country of multinational firm).

Offshoring penalizes low-skilled workers on the grounds that their work often involves easily offshored routine activities than jobs undertaken by high-skilled workers (Blinder, 2009; Geishecker & Görg, 2008). Supporting this view, Blinder (2009) indicated that about 25% of low-skilled American jobs are vulnerable to offshoring. However, as opined by Grossman and Ross-Hansberg (2008), though unskilled workers are vulnerable to offshoring, their wages may rise if the productivity effect associated with offshoring is sufficiently large as compared those of skilled workers. Similarly, Mitra and Ranjan (2010) argued that offshoring may increase productivity and consequences increase wages and decrease unemployment. Kohler and Smolka (2011) also contended that conditions exist under which the creation of jobs the following offshoring dominates the destruction of jobs even when productivity effects are at play. This finding suggests that one should analyze offshoring-productivity link to have a better understanding of offshore effects on labor markets.

Crino (2009) reviewed the literature on the effects of foreign activities of multinational firms and the offshoring activities on labor markets of developed countries. Study findings indicated that material offshoring increases the risk of job losses, as well as the elasticity of employment demands (Crino, 2009). In this way, material offshoring worsens the volatility of employment and wage inequality between unskilled and skilled workers. The study found that service offshoring changes the workforce composition in favor of high-skilled workers while exerting a small but significant negative impact on the total employment. The study further noted that multinational enterprises appear to substitute foreign and domestic labor as a response to changes in wages occurring in different countries globally (Crino, 2009). Crino observed that substitutability is weak and largely driven by multinational firms seeking direct investments.

Hummels et al. (2014) used data collected from Danish workers to style fact about exporting, offshoring, instruments that facilitate offshoring and the effects of offshoring on the labor market within the Danish context. Results showed that within the labour job market, while exporting increases wages of both high-skilled and low-skilled workers, offshoring increases high-skilled wage. However, the study found the net trade wage-effect to vary within the same skill-type, and wage-effect of offshoring to vary substantially across task characteristics.

Autor et al. (2013) assessed the impact of the increase in Chinese import competition on U.S. local labor markets between 1990 and 2007. The Autor et al. study exploited variations in the market and in import exposure originating from differences in specialization in the industry and instrumenting for imports to the United States. Findings showed that imports cause a reduction in wages in local labor markets, lower labor force participation, and higher unemployment. Autor et al. further opined that import competition account for one-quarter of an aggregate reduction in the manufacturing employment in the United States and that transfer benefits payments for healthcare, retirement, disability, and unemployment raise sharply in labor markets exposed to trade.

Bernard et al. (2018) studied the effects of offshoring on the allocation of resources by the firm across activities during the 2001-2006. Using detailed new data, the study provided a measure of offshoring, documented its relationship with the firms' trading decisions, and showed that offshoring enterprises tend to import the same products. The study also demonstrated that offshoring increases the growth of technology workers, and that reallocation of workers tends to be accompanied by an increase in the offshoring firm's R & D spending and product development.

Ghosh (2018) studied the offshoring as a productivity-enhancing activity within the Spain context. In this study, Ghosh

(2018) examined whether offshoring can lead to alteration in firm-level employment composition. Ghosh (2018) also sought to find out whether offshoring can lead to increased innovation expenditure, and take place in favor of high-skilled employees. Using firm-level microdata obtained from Spain's manufacturing sector, this study showed that offshoring positively impacts in high-skilled employment and R & D expenditures in Spain (Ghosh, 2018).

CHAPTER 10. OFFSHORING AND TECHNOLOGY INNOVATION

Impact of Offshoring on Innovation

Understanding the effects of offshoring on innovation is important because technological innovation is one of the drivers of economic growth (Baumol, 2002; Hira & Hira, 2005). As documented in the extant literature, innovation successfully takes place via a delicate balance in a system encompassing R & D units, suppliers, the financial system, and clients (Chapman & Corso, 2005; Mills, Schmitz, & Frizelle, 2004; Ricart et al., 2004).

Other studies indicated that firms often centralize R & D along with other core business activities in their home country at their headquarters (Cantwell & Narula & Michel, 2009; Piscitello, 2007). However, researchers reported an increasing trend in the internationalization of the inventive activities and R & D during the last forty years(Ambos & Ambos, 2011; Becker, Ekholm, & Muendler, 2013; Manning, Massini, &

Lewin, 2008). Ambos and Ambos (2011) argued that this trend is largely driven by the firms' need to source complementary competences, talents, and assets abroad, as well as to exploit existing home-based advantages. For Hummels et al. (2014) and others (e.g., Ernst, 2010), this practice of offshoring R & D activities is a way of the firms actualizing the phenomenon of Global Innovation Networks, where production and marketing departments and foreign and domestic R & D labs of non-multinational and multinational enterprises interact across and within firms' boundaries for the global diffusion and generation of innovation.

In general, this increase in offshoring activities raised fears that R & D offshoring may lead to the transfer of knowledge from developed countries to developing countries, consequently impacting on the competitiveness of advanced countries. The argument is that R & D offshoring may create the *hollowing* out risk. At the same time, other researchers suggested the contrary, that this process may be beneficial to home countries on the grounds that the process would foster growth and facilitate some reverse technology transfer at home. This chapter addresses this issue by discussing the extent to which offshoring may lead to *hollowing out* risk or foster growth and facilitate some reverse technology transfer at home.

Impact of Offshoring on Technology Innovation

The prevalent perspective in the academic literature is that offshoring affects the firms' innovative ability in the home location. There is also a concern in the greater public and academics that the R & D and engineering might follow the offshoring of manufacturing, and that this may jeopardize the home economies' ability to maintain their leadership and economic growth (Barnard, 2010; Horvit, 2004).

For example, Chapman and Corso (2005) support the first argument that R & D offshoring practices can potentially enhance the firms' innovating capability by expanding technology interaction and sourcing from different geographically dispersed suppliers with a view to augment their stock of knowledge. On the contrary, Narula and Zanfei (2005) support the argument that R & D and engineering follow the offshoring of manufacturing by advancing that offshoring firms tend to establish R & D labs abroad to effectively adapt to their services and products to the specificities and need of local markets. According to Piscitello and Rabbiosi (2006), these firms eventually decontextualize innovations designed for the local markets to become part of their knowledge base and proceed to exploit them elsewhere.

Similarly, Manning, Massini, and Lewin (2008) advanced that multinational firms offshore R & D with a view to gaining access to lower-cost highly qualified R & D personnel, as well as to access important inputs abroad such as technology and knowledge complementary to those established at home. However, in view of Narula and Zanfei (2005), offshoring of R & D may not necessarily translate into an increase in productivity and knowledge at home. Narula and Zanfei (2005) offered the following compelling arguments to qualify the statement that offshoring of R & D may not necessarily translate into an increase in productivity and knowledge at home.

First, the offshoring firms must have the ability to successfully manage research transfer of knowledge from offshored laboratories to the rest of the firm as well as transfer the knowledge back to the headquarters. This move may require firms to adopt sophisticated mechanisms for integrating and disseminating tacit and explicit knowledge. Second, offshore laboratories must be useful in extracting knowledge from foreign countries. For this to be achieved, firms need investments and time to facilitate them to establish relations with foreign actors (Narula & Michel, 2009). Castellani and Pieri (2014) confirmed that indeed these conditions must be met for the offshoring of R & D to translate into an increase in productivity and knowledge at home. Castellani and Pieri investigated the association between R & D offshoring and productivity dynamics in European firms. In particular, the study examined whether the impacts of R & D investments abroad differ from those in other business activities such as in manufacturing.

The findings revealed that offshoring regions report higher productivity gains suggesting that R & D offshoring affects regional productivity. However, the study (Castellani & Pieri, 2014) noted that these positive productivity effects fade down over time based on the number of projects carried out abroad. The study also estimated regressions of productivity gains as a function of the number of international R & D investments that lagged, while controlling for country fixed effects, a measure of inward FDIs, and other regional characteristics. Results showed a positive correlation between home region productivity gains and the level of R & D offshoring. This finding supported the argument that R & D offshoring strengthens the competitiveness of the home country. The study also found a positive association between inward investments and regional productivity growth.

Elsewhere, researchers suggested that R & D offshoring impacts on productivity at home by reallocating market shares and allowing firms to sell more, and that firms achieve this goal by adapting products or services to local needs and charging lower prices (Barba Navaretti, & Falzoni, 2010; Castellani & Zanfei, 2006; Elhaan, Melitz, & Yeaple, 2004; Grossman & Rossi-Hansberg, 2008). According to Helpman, Melitz, and Yeaple (2004), regional productivity would increase as a result of the firms increasing their market share provided firms engaging in offshoring are productive ones.

Supporting this subject, Castellani and Zanfei (2006) advanced that offshoring of R & D may also indirectly impact on the exit / entry, size, and productivity of other firms from the home region. According to Castellani, Jimenez, and Zanfei (2013), this mechanism is reflected in the spill over effects that occur as a result of inward Foreign Direct Investment (FDI). Castellani, Jimenez, and Zanfei (2013) further contented that by opening R & D labs abroad as part of the process of offshoring R & D, multinational enterprises may terminate activities in their home country. Therefore, these may disrupt linkages with local institutions and firms forcing them to exit the market. In contrast, where offshoring of R & D facilitates reverse of knowledge transfer, domestic firms may benefit from positive externalities, through inter-firm linkages, imitation, and labour mobility (Castellani et al., 2013).

Feenstra (2010) also found evidence linking the offshoring of R & D and reverse technology transfer using patent citation data from European firms. The findings of this study are further reinforced by result found by D'Agostino, Laursen, and Massini (2010) and Piscitello and Rabbiosi (2006) that patenting of R & D activities in OECD regions and countries gains from R & D offshoring activities in developing countries. As suggested by D'Agostino, Laursen, and Santangelo (2013), reverse transfer of technology from firms affiliated to the parent company in foreign countries to the home country parent firm may give these home countries and firms a competitive advantage particularly when complementarities exist between the offshore R & D and the home region. Similarly, Nieto and Rodriguez (2011) used firm-level data obtained from Spain to show that offshoring R & D is positively related to innovation performance. However, the effects of R & D offshoring were reportedly increased on product innovations than on process innovations.

Several mechanisms have been identified in international economics and business literature on how R & D offshoring affects home country economic activity. The first mechanism is that R & D offshoring alters the type of inputs and the nature of the task performed in the home country (Grossman & Rossi-Hansberg, 2006; Markusen, 2002). Offshoring enterprises focus on skill-intensive types of economic activities, such as coordinating, supervising, and other value addition auxiliary services and activities and technology in their home country. The consequence of these offshoring, activities at home of offshoring enterprises may become innovation intensive. As indicated by Barba, Navaretti and Falzoni (2004), this effect of offshoring may be increased and reinforced if offshoring is a zero-sum game and one that generates additional demand at the firm level, which also provides benefits to stages of production to firms at home. Second, offshoring may serve to argument innovation at the multinational firm's home country by enabling the firm to benefit from the transfer of technology and knowledge from affiliates in the foreign country back home (Castellani & Pieri, 2013; D'Agostino et al., 2013; Mihalache et al., 2012).

For example, Mihalache et al. (2012) demonstrated that offshoring and firm innovativeness have a U-inverted relationship suggesting that companies with a medium level of offshoring reported the highest level of innovativeness. However, Mihalache et al. observed that innovativeness as a benefit of offshoring diminishes beyond a certain threshold, emphasizing that beyond this threshold, offshoring may even hinder innovation. In a similar study, Crino (2009) assessed the effects of offshoring (imported inputs) on firms in Central Asia, Eastern, and Central Europe. The study findings suggested and between importing inputs a proxy of offshoring) and specialization in intensive and high-skill activities such as improvements in product quality R & D and technology adoption, and production of new goods. Similarly, using firms sampled from emerging economies, Fritsch and Görg (2013) found a positive relationship between offshoring and innovation. In a separate study, Karpaty and Tingvall (2011) demonstrated using Swedish multinational enterprises that offshoring negatively affects R & D intensity at home noting that effect is stronger when offshoring occurs in North America and other European countries. However, offshoring to developing countries has not to effect on the intensity of R & D. In another study involving Australian firms, Egger and Pfaffermayr (2009) reported a positive correlation between offshoring and higher investments in intangible assets and R & D at home countries. In the same vein, Mazzanti, Montresor, and Pini (2009) also reported a positive association between offshoring and variables that describe technological innovation.

Other studies that assessed the effects of offshoring on employment and skills in the home country also found evidence that offshoring is indirectly and positively associated with innovation (Hansson, 2005; Head & Ries, 2002). For example, Head and Ries (2002) found evidence that offshoring positively impacts on skill intensity at the home country, and that this effect is enhanced when offshoring moves towards emerging economies. Egger and Egger (2003) replicated these results using data from Eastern Europe by investigating whether offshoring services from Austria to Eastern Europe impacted on skill intensity. In this study, Egger and Egger found that offshoring leads to the changes in skill intensity for Austria firms that offshored their activities to Eastern Europe during the 1990s. In contrast, Slaughter (2000) did not find a statistically significant effect of offshoring on innovation for U.S. firms during the 1990s. These conflicting results from data obtained from firms in different firms may suggests that the effect of offshoring on innovation depends on the location where offshoring occurs.

There are also studies that suggested that offshoring negatively impacts on innovation. For example, in view of the firms' interactive processes, technological learning from production may be useful input for process and product innovation (Ketokivi & Ali-Yrkkö, 2009). Advancing this argument, Ketokivi and Ali-Yrkkö (2009) argued that the factory can function *as a laboratory*. Ketokivi and Ali-Yrkkö illustrated this analogy by advancing that offshoring of production activities to low-income countries may minimize technological learning from production, and cut many of these links, and thus generate less technological innovations at home. In the same vein, Naghavi and Ot-taviano (2009) suggested that offshoring may lead to reduced domestic innovation and reduced feedback from manufacturing firms offshore abroad, and consequently lead to a reduction in domestic product innovation.

Dachs eṭ al. (2014) used a dataset of manufacturing enterprises from European countries, the dataset on the process, product and organizational innovation, and a propensity value matching estimator to assess the causal effect of production offshoring on manufacturing firms' innovative capabilities in the home country. Result revealed that offshoring firms introduce more frequently new products, invest in advanced process technologies more frequently, and employ a higher share of design personnel and R & D than non-offshoring firms. No evidence supports concerns that production offshoring may hurt innovation as a result of lost links between product development and production.

Fifarek, Veloso, and Davidson (2008) also used patents in the high-tech area of rare element industry to examine the long-term effects of offshoring practices on the rate of technological innovation of home economies. The rationale for using this rare earth element in this study was that this area has evolved towards relocation to emerging economies and outsourcing. In this way, this rare earth industry could provide insights into potential long-term effects of offshoring on innovation. Using patent data to measure the innovative performance of rare earth technologies, Fifarek et al. demonstrated that material offshoring was significantly associated with a decrease in the rate of rare earth technology innovations among in the United States. These findings showed that a progressive loss of rare earth technology innovation is offshored by the U.S. firms. These findings also suggest that a strong offshoring trend in a firm's business environment may result in negative effects on their ability to innovate in their home market. Furthermore, these results suggest that offshoring benefits in efficient driven innovation, expanded markets or reduced prices, may be accompanied with a decline in innovation in certain areas.

Barba Navaretti, Castellani, and Disdier (2010) also found similar results using a survey of EU firms. Managers of firms interviewed in Barba, Navaretti, Castellani, and Disdier (2010) noted that firms benefited from R & D offshoring in several ways. First, R & D offshoring led to a reduction in the amount of time taken by firms to commercial an innovative product or idea. Second, the R & D offshoring facilitates managers to develop the ability to successfully choose R & D projects. Third, firms benefitted from the efficiency of the product innovation process. Last, the R & D offshoring facilitated firms to learn from other firms about their R & D. Other studies also provided evidence to show that offshoring R & D may reinforce firms' productivity and foster output growth.

Conclusion

In conclusion, there is literature on the effects of offshoring on R & D offshoring and innovation and productivity at home. Though, the results of these studies are mixed, most studies found evidence that R & D offshoring promotes growth and facilitates some reverse technology transfer at home. Overall, in view of the findings of these studies, offshoring of R & D affects the productivity at home of multinational firms through various transmission channels. However, only a few of these channels can be observed at the firm level. An aggregate perspective can facilitate the evaluation of the net effects of these effects. Therefore, regional level rather than country level channels can appropriately capture them.

CHAPTER 11.
BACK-SHORING

Keeping the Terminology Straight

In the policy discussions on back-shoring, different terms notably on-shoring, near-shoring, and re-shoring are used interchangeably. While some researchers see these terms as having the same meaning, others consider them as concepts that should be conceptualized differently. This chapter elucidates explores the use of these terms namely on-shoring, near-shoring, and re-shoring in their extant literature. The chapter further explores the trend in back-shoring within the global context and the American context.

On-shoring, Near-shoring, and Re-shoring

For Ellram, Tate, and Petersen (2013), re-shoring entails moving production/manufacturing back to the parent firm's country. Ellram et al. further noted that re-shoring is a reverse decision to the off-shoring decision involving the transfer of production activities from abroad to home country (back-shoring). According to Ellram et al., re-shoring may not necessarily translate to the closure or repatriation of all activities previously offshored by a company. For example, a U.S. multination may re-shore its production activities to Mexico or the United States from Singapore but continue with the production in Singapore to serve the regional or local market. In this way, Ellram et al. consider re-shoring to fundamentally involve locating production activities irrespective of the mode of ownership (i.e., outsourced to independent suppliers or performed in-house). Another typical example of re-shoring in this view is a German multinational moving the manufacturing of intermediates by external suppliers in China back to Germany.

In a separate study, Fratocchi et al. (2014) described reshoring as a change in location from the previous offshore country to the parent country. As described in the extant literature, back-shoring entails re-concentrating parts of production from foreign suppliers and own foreign locations to the company's domestic production (Kinkel & Maloca, 2009). For others, back-shoring typically entails relocating production activities from foreign country to the parent firm's home country (Arlbjørn & Mikkelsen, 2014; Fratocchi et al., 2014; Foerstl, Kirchoff, & Bals, 2016; Kinkel & Maloca, 2009). Also as reflected in the framework of theories of multinational companies, back-shoring is a reverse decision of an offshoring decision made by a multinational (Bals et al., 2013; Gray et al., 2013; Tate, 2014; Ellram et al., 2013). According to Arlbjørn and Mikkelsen (2014), back-shoring may originate from foreign suppliers, as well as from the firm's wholly owned production sites. The former form of back-shoring is referred to as outsourcing back-shoring while the latter is referred to as captive back-shoring. For other researchers, back-shoring entails geographic re-location of the company's functional value creating operations from foreign countries back to the parent country

(Holz, 2009). Thus, in general, reshoring refers to the change in location from the previous offshore country to the parent country.

On-shoring slightly differs from the near- / back-re-shoring concepts entailing that the company locating production activities from a faraway market to a close to market demand. In this way, on-shoring may also refer to re-shoring especially within the context of a company engaging in moving production when motivated by its proximity to the demand market. On-shoring may also be considered a form of off-shoring when a U.S. multination moves its new production activities in Singapore in response to the growing and large demand in Singapore. Near-shoring, as described in the academic literature, refers to the company's decision to re-locate activities that were previously offshored to the country that boarder the company's parent country. For example, Klier (2015) advanced that Mexico is an attractive country for U.S. companies' offshoring activities because of its proximity to the U.S. market. This proximity gives Mexico flexibility. Similarly, Bogar and Holmes (2013) suggests that low labor costs, close proximity to the United States, changes in trade policy, and improvements in infrastructure and training have contributed to Mexico's attractiveness to the U.S. multinational companies that offshore their production. Desai, Foley, and Hines (2009) reinforced this view that Mexico has significantly improved its manufacturing cost structure including exchange rates, energy costs, labor productivity, and wage costs, and that it is about 4% cheaper than China when it comes to manufactured goods. Other terms that feature commonly in the re-shoring discussion is internationalization / de-globalization and international divestment.

In general, the concepts of near-shoring, back-shoring, and re-shoring all refer to the reverse of offshoring. Accordingly, these terms (re-shoring, back-shoring, and near-shoring) are used interchangeably in this chapter to refer to back-shoring.

A Growing Attention for Back-shoring / Re-shoring

Although off-shoring persists in the international business practice, a counter trend has been observed since 1980s whereby multinational firms that previously offshored their production are adopting regionally-based location strategy or move their operations back to home from abroad (Ellram et al., 2013). According to Ellram et al. (2013), this practice may have been informed by a noticeable trend of few multinational firms engaging in back-shoring. For example, as demonstrated by Dachs and Zanier (2015) between 2012 and 2015, 4% of multinational firms in Europe were reported to have engaged in back-shoring. This figure was considerably lower than 17% of the multinational firms that offshoring their production activities abroad. However, for Kinkel (2012), back-shoring as a concept is not a new phenomenon as companies have always engaged in decisions to move production activities to the parent country from abroad largely motivated by disappointing experiences with manufacturing abroad. Kinkel added that back-shoring spans sectors and industries that are heterogeneous in technology and knowledge content.

Supporting this view, Fratocchi et al. (2016) advanced that back-shoring was first highlighted in the popular press, and that this growing trend of back-shoring may suggest that companies are abandoning the past integrated production and international strategies in favor of global production value chain networks. Fratocchi et al. further indicated that outsourcing and offshoring have resulted in global value chains (GVCs) by transforming nationally based manufacturing sectors of the past decades. Fratocchi et al. further emphasized that the phenomenon of back-shoring does not denote the end of off-shoring.

Back-shoring is picking up as the off-shoring continues to take place with current evidence suggesting that companies still consider off-shoring to be important (Fratocchi et al., 2016). According to Fratocchi et al. (2016), large firms in Europe tend to engage in back-shoring more than small firms do, and at the industry level, back-shoring is lowest in the industry such as manufacturing of beverages and food, wood, bricks and glass, clothing and other low-technology industries. In contrast, high-technology industries, including a computer, telecom equipment, pharmaceuticals, electrical equipment, and transport industries report frequent back-shoring activities. According to Dachs and Zanker (2015), India, China, the United States, Germany, and other new EU member states are the main source of back-shoring. Collectively these countries accounted for a fifth of all the back-shoring activities that occurred in Europe between 2012 and 2015 (Dachs, & Zanker, 2015). However, worth noting is that following years of large-scale outsourcing and offshoring, multinational firms seems to be increasingly considering other options for structuring their production processes and more diversified sourcing strategies.

CHAPTER 12. BACK-SHORING: DRIVERS

Motivations Behind Back-shoring

In the empirical question dominating the scholarly debate on back-shoring is "why company re-shores their production back home?" Like the analysis of drivers of off-shoring, the analysis of motivations of re-shoring is of great importance because it may provide insight to policy makers and researchers as to whether these de-internalization patterns can be considered "goal-oriented and purposeful" (Benito, 2015, p. 12). Moreover, understanding why companies re-shore may provide insight into value activities that are involved in re-shoring, how these activities are governed, and where they are located (Benito, 2015). In addition, understanding the motivations for re-shoring may help determine whether the political and economic debates on popular media platforms influence companies to engage in re-shoring or whether these motivations are largely informed by other factors.

The Rationale for Re-shoring

A wealth of different back-shoring drivers has been proposed in the extant academic literature (Bals, Kirchoff, & Foerstl, 2016; Foerstl, Kirchoff, & Bals, 2016; Fratocchi et al., 2016; Stentoft et al., 2016). The hypothesis that commonly features in most studies on re-shoring is that companies engage in re-shoring as a strategy to correct managerial errors such as knowledge of the off-shore location and insufficient planning (Kinkel & Maloca, 2009). Other researchers consider re-shoring as a reverse of a rational off-shoring decision driven by changes and contingencies in the home country or offshore environment, such as lower energy costs in the United States and Europe, or rising costs of ownership in countries such as China (Martiez-Mora & Merino, 2014; Tate et al., 2014). For other scholars, back-shoring follows the firms' inability to solve complex challenges arising from offshore production (Simchi-Levi et al., 2012; Manning, 2014).

Other scholars view back-shoring as driven by consumers' pressure on companies with pressure believed to originate from perception that western productions have higher quality than emerging countries' production (Ancarani et al., 2015; Fratocchi et al., 2016; Grappi, Romani, & Bagozzi, 2015; Tate et al., 2014; Robinson & Hsieh, 2016; Martinez-Mora & Merino, 2014). The heterogeneity of drivers of re-shoring suggests that several back-shoring topologies may influence companies into considering re-shoring possibly influenced by various factors notably the company's dimension, its strategic focus, its internalization path, and the industry (Foerstl et al., 2016). However, with some exceptions, researchers largely examined the drivers underlying re-shoring by analyzing the form of off-shoring that caused them (Gylling et al., 2015; Joubioux & Vanpoucke, 2016). This seems to be contrary to the view that back-shoring is related to the offshoring process: why the company previously off-shored the activities; where and when it off-shored the activities; and to whom it delegated these activities (Joubioux & Vanpoucke, 2016).

Nonetheless, the re-shoring debate seems to fundamentally reduce itself to the discussion of countries' attractiveness to investment as it is concerned with where the production takes place. As suggested by OECD (2011) a multitude of factors including the growth and size of the regional/local market, the availability of resources, wage (costs), the presence of scientific infrastructure and suppliers, and human capital play a role in the firm's decision to locate activities. These location factors are known to vary in importance along the value chain (R & D, distribution, production, etc.) and across activities and industries. The gaining of the importance of re-shoring may suggest that developed economies are increasingly becoming attractive to some of the previously off-shoring production activities. Several reasons have been highlighted in the extant literature to explain why location factors in advanced economies have become relatively attractive to production activities. These reasons may be considered *realities* or myths based on the view that considerable disagreements exist among researcher in relation to the importance of the back-shoring phenomenon.

Changing Structure in Cost in Emerging Economies

During the 1990s and 2000s many firms off-shored their production activities to low-cost emerging economies (OECD, 2013). Consequently, production costs in these emerging economies increased significantly. For example, an average hourly wage in China increased by between 15-20% per year since the 1990s leading to the erosion of cost advantage achieved by companies especially in labor-intensive production activities (World Economic Forum, 2012). This reinforces the report by World Economic Forum (2012) that the average hourly wage in most emerging countries increased significantly from 2% of the U.S. average hourly wage to in 2000 to 9% in 2015. The building costs and energy costs in some emerging countries also rose dramatically from the 1990s through 2000s. Some skeptical economic analysts downplay these wage increases by arguing that these wage increases have been offset by productivity increases (Ozawa, 2008). Ozawa (2008) and other researchers (e.g., Nager & Atkinson, 2015) further advanced that within the context of the "flying Geese patterns", firms seeking low labor costs tend to invest in countries and regions considered to be of low cost. However, worth noting is that though these emerging economies lack the supply networks, transportation infrastructure, and lower productivity and skills in their labor force. In addition, it is worth noting that there are other factors besides labor costs that influence companies' decision to invest onshore new production activities or continue existing production in these emerging economies and their decisions to notable factors include the growth and size of the local market

Growth in Manufacturing Digitalization in Emerging Economies

Emerging digital innovations and technologies such as data analytics, machine-to-machine communication (M2M), artificial intelligence and sensors gradually transformed production in emerging economies. Some researchers argue that the increasing use of these new technologies has made labor costs less important as a source of competitive advantage to companies in developed economies. For example, some argue that the growing use of robots and other automation of production processes have eroded labor cost advantage enjoyed by multinational companies from emerging economies. This growing digitalization is also thought to allow for high-quality and low-cost production in emerging economies, ultimately favoring re-shoring and discouraging off-shoring from these economies (OECD, 2015). Some results from OECD (2015) shows a negative relationship between off-shoring and robot use across industries and countries.

Underestimation and Miscalculation of "Full Costs"

Operational, logistical, and management problems have in some cases been blamed for making off-shoring unprofitable and led to significant "hidden" costs (Boston Consulting Group, 2014; Porter & Rivkin, 2012). The high pecuniary cost of coordination, communication, and monitoring between headquarters and distance affiliates of companies are also believed to influence companies to consider back-shoring.

Production, Innovation, and Co-location of R & D

Arguments have been advanced that co-location between activities along the value chain plays a role in back-shoring. For example, discussing the role of co-location in back-shoring, Pisano and Shih (2009) argued that in several industries including the engineering industries separation of production from innovative and R & D activities may slow down innovation.

According to Pisano and Shih, in some off-shoring activities, feedback affects between product and innovation changes and activities in the value chain tend to be not easier to manage in a long supply chain leading to slower rates of innovation, which in turn hollows out the company's competitive advantage. Pisano and Shih further advanced that some companies back-shored their production activities back home to offset other risks associated with off-shoring of innovation and R & D activities.

Off-shoring as a Potential Threats to Intellectual Property

When engaging in off-shoring of innovative activities to emerging economies, some companies learn that intellectual protection protections enforcement differs from their home country. This insight reinforced with the fear that local suppliers may gain understand their production process and become competitors influence these companies to make decisions to back-shore production back to their home countries. As indicated by Nager and Atkinson (2015), less developed legal systems for protecting intellectual property rights and weaker enforcement of these rights influence some companies to reconsider their decision to off-shore production to emerging economies and move some of their production activities back home.

Balancing Risk Dispersion and Costs Savings

The spreading of operations in other countries has made companies more vulnerable to disruptions from unexpected natural and man related risk events such as political unrest and natural disasters. Supply chains have become extensive and complex to the extent that any breakdown may have significant detrimental impacts on the supply chain of companies that off-shore their production activities (OECD, 2013). Natural events such as the floods in Thailand in 2011, the eruption of the volcano in Iceland in 2012, and the tsunami / earthquake in Japan in 2011 have demonstrated to companies that GVCs are highly fragile. To diversity risks and improve the resilience of supply chains, sometimes companies consider adding some redundancy by considering alternative GVCs and shorter GVCs, as well as bringing production to countries closer to their home countries.

Proximity to the Market to Achieve Flexibility

Researchers have linked back-shoring to proximity to markets, identified in the academic literature as a caused by attractive of emerging economies and that companies are seeking international investment when making decisions as to whether to off-shore or re-shore. The attractiveness of the emerging economies may be explained by the strong growth of these countries' markets and large size. The complexity and length of GVCs also appear to be exposing firms to large supply chain risks making them less flexible in responding to changing consumer preferences and demand. Companies appear to turn to a regional rebalancing of GVCs to achieve distributed and varied topography of production. This can be seen in the increasing evidence of the concentration of local/regional hubs in both emerging and developed economies closer to end markets. In addition, changes in technologies, demand factors, and cost structures may be contributing to manufacturing and production becoming more regional. For some products, long value chains, and product low labor costs are important competitive advantages. For other products, production tends to be organized at the regional rather than global level.

Advantages believed to influence companies to bring production in markets that are within the home country's proximity are faster time to the market and shorter lead times. Companies dealing in fashioned and customized products are required to deliver new products to customers on short notice, as well as respond promptly to the changing demand. The agility and flexibility are believed to be ignored by many companies that make the decision to offshore as these companies tend to be largely driven by the cost savings. Companies seek to gain flexibility in their processes by moving production centers in countries close to the home countries (i.e., closer to end markets).

The Oil / Shale Gas Resolution in the United States and a Weakening Dollar

The increasing recognition of the importance of shale gas in the United States and the weakening dollar play a role in influencing companies to engage in back-shoring to the United States. In particular, evidence Casson (2013) suggested that the re-shoring activities in chemical, fertilizer, cement and other energy-intensive industries is largely contributed by the dropping costs of energy, which is believed to be contributed by the increased availability of tight oil and shale gas as well as the rising costs of energy in emerging countries. On the contrary, the impact of the availability on re-shoring activities is reported to be low in industries in which energy costs constitute a relatively smaller proportion of the total cost of production.

Other drivers of re-shoring are identified as back-shoring drivers cost advantages, transaction cost advantage, maintaining control, market and knowledge seeking (Casson, 2013; Rugman, Verbeke, & Nguyen, 2011). Through, the lens of Dunning's (1988) eclectic paradigm and international theory, back-shoring is driven by internalization and location advantages from international production, changes in ownership, and a consequence of the firm's wrong assessment of offshoring associated advantages (as cited in Casson, 2013; Ellram et al., 2013; Fratocchi et al., 2016).

Foerstl, Kirchoff, and Bals (2016) classified back-shoring motivators according to Organizational Buying Behavior (OBB) and Transaction Cost Economics (TCE) theories. In this study, Foerstl et al. identified 29 motivations for back-shoring classified into two-level framework: behavioural human drivers, transactional drivers for back-shoring;

Foerstl et al. (2016) discussed the behavioural and human drivers for back-shoring from the perspective of bounded rationality. In view of bounded rationality, environmental complexities inherently limit choices made by decision makers by straining the bounds of knowledge and making it difficult for them to rationalize all possible outcomes and foresee all expected contingencies of supplier-buyer relationship (Cabral, Quelin, & Maia, 2013; Lewin, Massini, & Peeters, 2009). As advanced by Fredriksson and Jonsson (2009), the decision makers' inability to accurately foresee the performance outcomes of a project may cause the firm to report higher than expected outsourcing / offshoring related costs, as well as other negative outcomes such as excess monitoring and coordination of problem, suppliers dependence, and poor quality. Foerstl et al. advanced that some firm that engages in back-shoring tend to be influenced by these higher than expected outsourcing / offshoring related costs.

Supporting this view, Gray et al. (2013) observed that a multinational firm may be influenced to engage in back-shoring as a result of losing control over suppliers from abroad who act opportunistically to create serious reputational and financial costs associated with product recalls and defects. A typical example of bounded rationality within the back-shoring context as highlighted in Foerstl et al. (see Fratocchi et al., 2014), was the decision made by General Electric to invest in a production site in Kentucky-previously abandoned site outsourced/ offshored overseas- with a view to revitalizing the U.S. appliance production. General Electric's decision was informed by the unforeseen increase in labour costs in the Chinese market and a decline in sales that resulted from unpredictable product quality problems. In view of the General Electric's case, Foerstl et al. argued that the inability of the firm to take advantage of expected benefits, industry-contextual factors and the advent of unanticipated costs influence managers of multinational firms to reconsider offshoring decisions. The bandwagon effect cited as an outcome of decision-making biases by multinational firms is another product of bounded rationality. In this sense, some firms are believed to fail to obtain the benefits of offshoring and turn to back-shoring on grounds that they take on offshoring to imitate competitor outsourcing/offshoring decisions.

In line with this argument, Tate (2014) advanced that changes in managerial assessment by multinational firms may drive back-shoring decisions. According to Tate, managers of multinational firms may be influenced by managerial valuation and a shift in priorities towards different key performance metrics to reconsider the offshoring decisions in of back-shoring.

Veltri, Saunders, and Kavan (2008) also reinforced this view by indicating that a firm may reconsider its offshoring decision upon revisiting its previous decisions based on revised or new performance appraisal system. For example, backshore-insourcing may be by changes in the firm's market-product combinations. Varta Microbattery GmbH demonstrated that a firm change in a firm's market-product combinations may drive it to revert to back-shoring by changing their product-market strategy. In this sense, Varta embraced micro battery and abandoned heavy industrial batteries. To solve the problem of the short product lifecycle in this product segment, Varta turned to back-shoring to enable it closely integrate production and product development at its premises headquartered in Germany. This example demonstrates how the context in which insourcing and re-shoring decisions may be influenced by firm objectives and strategy. Additionally, the example also highlights how managers perceive drivers of insourcing and re-shoring.

For Gulbrandsen, Sandvik, and Haugland (2009) the transfer of firms' knowledge to their suppliers and subsidiaries may be complicated by lack of knowledge codification. According to Gulbrandsen et al., difficulties experienced by a firm in disseminating relevant knowledge to subsidiaries to facilitate value creation may enhance transaction costs consequently favoring back-shoring. Problems in knowledge dissemination are also negatively associated with the use of external partners, and this favors back-shoring. A typical example that demonstrates the knowledge dissemination problem as a driver of re-shoring is the production facility of Otis Elevator in Mexico that experienced a production backlog and prompted the cancelation of orders. In this case, Otis Elevator, which had offshored its production to benefit from the comparatively low cost of labor and government incentives decided to re-shore production from Mexico to South Carolina. The managers of Otis Elevator claimed that their decision to re-shore production was informed by the idea that specific knowledge was embedded among R & D, sales and production in South Carolina. The managers of Otis Elevator claimed that failure by the firm's managers to communicate on client-specific matters with the Mexican subsidiary led to high capital lock-up and rework leading to the accumulation of transaction costs that justified the firm's decision to re-shore its initiative. This example demonstrated that the viability of the firm's decision to re-shore may be influenced by the capabilities of the firm.

Opportunism is one of the drivers of back-shoring. As described by Foerstl et al. (2016), opportunism reflects the actors' behavior towards partners involved in a transaction with self-interest as the key driver. In such an arrangement, both parties engage in information seeking activities based on the assumption that other transaction partners would act opportunistically. This act of engaging in information seeking activities by firms acting opportunistically may alter inter-firm relationships leading to increased transaction costs (Handley & Benton, 2013). According to Handley and Benton (2013), opportunism typical causes dissatisfied buying firms and leads to high control costs and coordination.

Opportunism is also believed to lead to de-prioritization of business relationships prompting firms to seek insourcing and re-shoring alternatives (Handley & Benton, 2013). Handley and Benton further advanced that offshoring multinational enterprises my become dependent on external suppliers for assets, technology and other forms of resources that increase the risk of opportunism on the part of the supplier as well as shift the relational power towards the supplier. For example, as highlighted in Re-shoring Initiative (2015), perceived risks associated with the availability of suppliers and reliance on supplies' possession of resources to dictate prices of materials influenced Hubbardton Forge-a manufacturer of lamp fixture, to re-shore components sourced to the United States. from China.

Transactional Drivers

Firms tend to experience potential disturbances as a result of environmental uncertainty. Such environmental uncertainty causes unpredictability and volatility in the marketplace. As such, it is considered one of the drivers of contemporary insourcing and re-shoring decisions (Tate et al., 2014; Ellram et al., 2013). Sirkin, Zinser, and Rose (2014) further emphasized that environmental uncertainty factors including previously unforeseen costs increases notably transportation and fuel costs and wage rates may disrupt business models influencing firms to consider re-shoring. In addition, macroeconomic changes such as exchange rate fluctuations, raw material shortages, and economic growth projects may also induce uncertainty in the market influencing the decision to re-shore and inshore (Lewin et al., 2009; Tate et al., 2014). This view that environmental uncertainty may influence the back-shoring decision was demonstrated by Lemken GmbH, and Co.KG, which re-shored its assembly of machinery from the Russian subsidiary to the supplier in Germany, its home country. This decision was arguably a reaction to high logistical uncertainty from export regulation, energy costs, volatile material, and political instability in Russia.

Regulatory and institutional changes including labor market

regulations, policy changes and subsidies, political stability, and tax structures also believed to affect the attractiveness of certain regions and countries and are identified as sources of uncertainty (Gray et al., 2013; Tate & Ellram, 2009). Changes to security assurances by the government such as intellectual property protections are also reported to impact on multinational firms' decision in favor of insourcing and reshooting decisions (Tate, 2014). In this vein, the decision by Caterpillar to re-shore its manufacturing of compact engine from Japan to Texas, United States was influenced by loosening intellectual property protection and increasing unfavorable and unpredictable tax policies in Japan.

Supply chain complexity is another constituent of uncertainty (Ellram et al., 2013; Tate, Dooley, & Ellram, 2011). According to Ellram et al. (2013) horizontal complexity (e.g., tiers), geographic length, and dispersion of supply chain and vertical complexity (direct suppliers) are believed to create uncertainty for firms that engage in offshoring influencing their decision to consider re-shoring and in-shoring. Reinforcing this view, Lewin et al. (2009) noted that supply chain complexities increase control and coordination efforts and costs thereby increasing transportation costs. In another study, Lieb and Lieb (2009) demonstrated that supply chain complexity impacts on firms' decision to backshore. In this study, Lieb and Lieb reported that one-fourth of companies in Western countries re-shored their services back to their home country to reduce the length of the supply chain. This means that firms' decision to backshore is driven by the need to simplify the complex supply chain.

Psychic and cultural distances are also linked to supply chain complexity (Handley & Benton, 2013). In this vein, the prioritization of social and environmental concerns by multinational firms may be influenced by indifferences in some countries or regions versus others (Reuter et al., 2010). For example, Margarete Steiff GmbH found Insourcing-Near-shore production to be more attractive upon realizing that auditing was associated with high costs, and that there were environmental and labor practices issues with suppliers from China. This example also highlights how the firm's experiences and internal capabilities influence insourcing and re-shoring decisions in relation to the state of governance and location.

Task uncertainty is also reported to impact on outsourcing and offshoring decisions (Manuj & Mentzer, 2008; Handley & Benton, 2013). According to Handley and Benton (2013), technological and innovation progress in production technology may allow firms to shift to production modes considered to be less labor intensive and favor insourcing and re-shoring. For example, as pointed out by Lasi et al. (2014), the technological and innovation progress towards versatile automatic operations facilitated manufacturing cells to autonomously and independently optimize and control manufacturing without requiring human intervention. Similarly, this technological and innovation development enable NCR to produce ATM closer to its sales markets as its relocated value creation from Asia to Hungary to serve its closer European markets. Furthermore, production process and task scale inter-connectedness impacted on the firm's control intensity and coordination of transactions because the firm reported a significant reduction in coordination cost and effort between logistic and production and R & D functions (Ketokivi & Ali-Yrkkö, 2009).

Another example of task uncertainty reflecting the volume of transactions between parties involved in offshoring is the frequency of the anticipated transactions. According to Safizadeh, Field, and Ritzman (2008), when transactions do not reach expected scale and frequency with offshoring business partners, low fixed costs, and high logistics costs digression leads to less competitive cost positions than to alternatives centered at the regional level. This view was demonstrated by Lieb and Lieb (2009) that 57% of 3PLs's major customers shifted their manufacturing plants from India and China to Eastern Europe, Central America, and North America and that this move was aimed at dealing with the increased need to deal with smaller lot sizes and for customization. In addition, frequent changes in the design of components and products increase the novelty of the task, and in turn increase the interconnectedness of R & D, internal operations, and downstream and upstream functions, as well as increase pre-transaction costs. Task frequency is also believed to increase with the increase in the variety of product leading to high costs for offshoring / outsourcing tasks (McIVor, 2009).

Asset specificity, as indicated by Mclvor (2009), describes durable investments designed for specific processes and products. According to Mclvor, in a dedicated transaction, customized assets can reduce market adaptability and product variety as well as lower transaction costs demand for a certain product or service changes. For instance, if the suppliers' production technology or product no longer suits the product architecture of the firm or becomes outdated, the focal firm may seek regional sources in an attempt to integrate the activity in-house or change the supplier (Ciarli et al., 2008; Handley & Benton, 2013). In this sense, the context of innovative and technological advances may impact on how asset specificity affects the firm's decision-making. This idea was reflected in Siteco

GmbH decision to backshore the manufacturing of its high efficiency bubs from Slovenia to Germany. Siteco GmbH made this change in response to the shift in a product technology that required greater product customization but with low demand for labor. In this case, reduced coordination and rework efforts favored final assembly and production in Germany. Thus, the comparative cost advantages afforded by the Slovenia plant eroded and necessitated the re-shoring of production of high efficiency bulbs. Another constituent of asset specificity is resource availability (Ellram et al., 2013). As indicated by Tate et al. (2014), intangible resources affect the strength of the commitment of the firm to outsourcing and offshoring decisions.

Perceived and known scarcity may influence a firm to reconsider governance and locational choices where it can exercise less partner dependence and have greater control of resources. For example, Wal-Mart decided to insource portions of its supply chain programs and infrastructure from different providers of logistics services to minimize its supplier dependence, safeguard its logistical capabilities, and demonstrate the impact of a change in the firm's strategies and objectives on its decisions. Last, human asset specificity resulting from investing in personnel dedicated to existing or new production efforts and product development may impact on the firm's decision to re-shore its services or products back home (Gulbrandsen, Sandvik, & Haugland, 2009; Ketokivi & Ali-Yrkkö, 2009). For instance, knowledge specificity, which is known to impact on human asset specificity, is associated with functional interdependence such as integration of R & D (Handley & Benton, 2013). Multinational firms such as Varta Microbattery GmbH, OtisInc., and Ford Motors indicate that from sales and production and colocation engineering after they insourced or back-shored, they noted enhance knowledge sharing, which resulted in enhanced security supply and reduced capital lock-up associated with reduced transaction costs.

In another study, Fratocchi et al. (2016) categorized drivers of re-shoring based on two variables: the predominant factors impacting on *level of analysis* or back-shoring decision (internal to the firm versus relating to the firm's external environment), and the firm's strategic goal (i.e., improving cost-efficiency versus increasing customer perceived value). This framework, as described by Fratocchi et al., is grounded in strategic management theories and international business theories. Using this framework, Fratocchi et al. advanced that perceived value goals of customers may explain the firm's decision to reshore its activities: its need to protect, maintain, and improve the critical attributes such as product innovation and perceived quality that drive customer value and customer services (Lindic & da Silva, 2011; Stringfellow, Teagarden, & Nie, 2008). In contrast, cost-efficiency goals may explain the firm's decision to relocate in pursuit of production cost advantage stemming from lower monitoring costs, higher productivity or lower labor costs, psychic distance, lower inventories, shorter logistics lead times, and automation (Robinson & Hsieh, 2016).

In view of Robinson and Hsieh (2016), TCE, International Trade Theory, and other theoretical approaches suggest that firms' decision to engage in back-shoring is driven by reduced gaps in costs of input between the offshore location and home location, and the high costs involved in coordinating distant relationships and operations. Other empirical studies were undertaken within the EU context confirmed through the theoretical perspectives of international trade theory, TCE and other theoretical approaches that factors such as reduced gaps in input costs between home location and offshore locations influence firms to re-shore activities from abroad to home countries (Handley, 2012). From example, from the international trade theoretical perspective, Handley (2012) advanced that firms that considered re-shoring faced a different reality to what they expected notably unintended consequences and indirect and direct hidden costs. As highlighted by Gulbrandsen, Sandvik, and Haugland (2009), direct costs included travel costs, additional investments in devices and machines, translation costs, additional costs associated with late delivery, and payment of bribes. Indirect costs as highlighted by Ketokivi and Ali-Yrkkö (2009) included low productivity, exchange rate risk, quality problems, indirect labor costs, and additional stocking costs, and cultural differences.

For other researcher, reasons for back-shoring vary from country to country. Within the Germany context, reasons for firms' back-shoring ranged from quality control problems to high shipping costs, productive factors and others. Factors associated with high shipping costs were highlighted as problems with funds transfers and international payments; reduced flexibility by firms to respond to ever changing conditions in the market; higher than anticipated warehousing and quality assurance costs; and difficulties experienced in training workers to obtain acceptable quality standards (Fraunhofer Institute for Systems & Innovation Research (ISI), as cited in Tate (2014). Other reasons cited for back-shoring by German companies include logistics, rising production costs, exchange rate fluctuations, unsatisfactory quality control, costs of productive factors (capital customs problems along the border, materials and labor, materials problems), banking problems, foreign ingredients negatively affected product taste, infrastructure capacity constraints, coordination and communication costs, and transportation costs. Notable German companies that engaged in back-shoring included Bellicon; Friatec; Hirschmann; Jungheinrich; Lemke; Katjes; Ritter-Sport; Steiff; Stiebel Eltron; Vorwerk; and Weigelt. Products re-shored by these companies included mini trampolines; Forklifts; electrical cables and connectors; industrial valves; candy; farm equipment; teddy bears; chocolates; water heaters; vacuum cleaners; and injection molding machines (ISI; Wissenschaftliche Studien zu Rückverlagerungen 2006).

Emphasizing the drivers of repatriation among German *tech* firms, Hameri and Hintsa (2009) hinted that when these companies offshore production abroad, they entrust their valuable intellectual property to people who have not a firm grasp of the intellectual property concept. Furthermore, these firms leave proprietary production methods in people who do not share a loyalty to the firm like people in home countries who devote their time on developing and perfecting these production methods. Within the UK context, Tate (2014) found that 14% of manufacturing firms that offshored their production abroad in 2008 and 2009 re-shored them to the UK. Reasons highlighted for back-shoring by these firms included rising logistics costs and product quality (Outsource Portfolio Blog, 2010). As indicated in this study, offshoring drives up wages in host countries consequently reducing the lower cost labor advantage. UK manufacturing firms were also concerned about the financial health of suppliers to overseas plants.

Drivers of back-shoring among firms in France appear somewhat similar to those cited by German firms: cost concerns; lack of internal competence; and quality concerns (Clever Age, 2006). A literature search about offshoring back-shoring in Spain showed that firms in Spain lagged German, UK, and France firms in back-shoring. Although Spain has one of the highest GDP among the EU countries, Spanish companies are believed to lack less incentive to backshore or offshore services or products in order to achieve lower labor costs (Agnese & Ricart Costa, 2009). Spanish Firms surveyed by Agnese and Ricart Costa (2009) about possible offshoring indicated that their key concerns were cultural differences, customer acceptance, and corporate resistance.

Other studies indicated that multiple factors play a role in the firms' decision to locate and relocate activities abroad and back home, including the growth of regional and local market (i.e., wage costs); human capital; the availability of resources; scientific infrastructure; and the presence of suppliers (OECD, 2011). These location factors are reported to vary along the value chain (distribution, R & D, production, etc.) across activities and industries.

CONCLUSION: OUTSOURCING VS. OFFSHORING: BUSINESS AND PSYCHOLOGY PERSPECTIVES

Companies have used global off-shoring phenomenon since the 1950s. The first wave of off-shoring took place post-World War II. During this phase, companies held onto their core functions and aspects of the production activities that gave the firm identity. Labor-intensive operations were outsourced to offshore facilities abroad. The emergence of internet technologies marked an important milestone in the off-shoring realm as it facilitated firms to eliminate the physical distance barrier allowing them to outsource new product manufacturing and development to suppliers across the globe. To gain access to ideas and talents from foreign business partners and reduce costs, company leaders started engaging in outsourcing production globally. This phenomenon also influenced firms to relocate high-value functions, including engineering, R & D and design functions abroad. In this way, many companies in different industries in developed economies started outsourcing their production abroad to their off-shore facilities.

From the business perspective, drivers or motivators of off-shoring as approached from different theoretical perspectives are efficiency (cost reduction); exploitation (developing foreign markets); and exploration (access to talented and knowledge people). From the empirical perspective, drivers of offshoring can be categorized as: ownership advantages, location advantages, and externalization advantages. Ownership drivers are technological capabilities and resources and international experience in other countries. Location-specific drivers include efficiency-seeking and capability-seeking drivers. Externalizations drivers to off-shoring include technological uncertainty and tacit knowledge drivers. Other drivers of off-shoring are identified as a company seeking to gain core competencies, cost reduction, opportunity to gain relevant specialized knowledge and skills, flexibility from external suppliers, and competitive pressure. Leaders of these companies were motivated by various factors to engage in off-shoring.

These motives can be collapsed into two categories: horizontal motives (better market access) and vertical motive (lower production costs. The horizontal motive seems to have more traction than vertical motive, especially where high trade barriers exist. However, the vertical motive may be more appealing when trade barriers decline. Horizontal relocation is favored by companies that seek to jump high trade barriers in order to access markets in other markets. High trade barriers may serve as a hindrance to global fragmentation of production. While both vertical and horizontal motives involve a certain level of relocating jobs between foreign production and domestic production sites, the term "off-shoring" as used within the realm of the public debate typically denotes the relocation of intermediate stages of supply value chain abroad with the ultimate goal of serving domestic customers. The idea behind this concept is that by lowering trade barriers, off-shoring promotes more vertical relocation than horizontal relocation. In this sense, companies tend to readily understand horizontal relocation as a necessary experience worth undergoing in order to achieve the goal of penetrating foreign markets. In contrast, as long customers are domestic, critics of off-shoring are more likely to see vertical relocation as opportunistic behavior to the disadvantage of domestic suppliers and workers.

From the psychology perspective, drivers of offshoring include costs and personal benefits such as possible loss or gain of attractive jobs / tasks by an organization. As demonstrated in this study, companies are justified to make an off-shoring decision as offshoring facilitates the relocation of production abroad facilitating the trade in intermediate services and goods across borders. Evidence from the sectorial studies and firm-level studies show that off-shoring has a limited negative impact on sector-level employment rather it benefits the domestic labor market. However, worth noting is that the effect of offshoring on domestic employment appears to be more complicated than using foreign workers as a replacement of domestic ones. The wider view and most common view on the effects of offshoring is that it allows firms to tap into cheap foreign employment and thus harming domestic workers. However, while offshoring production may have a direct displace impact on domestic workers, it may have an indirect effect on raising the demand for domestic workers through facilitating the increasing in overall production.

Evidence from the extant literature also shows that offshoring can enhance productivity by (a) accompanying restructuring measures which minimize inefficiencies; (b) lead to a static efficiency gain; (c) facilitates interactions between internal and foreign suppliers allowing firms to benefit from learning externalities; (d) raise profits and lower the marginal production costs of developing and low-wage countries may and create resources for investing in R & D; and (e) induce selection effects and tougher competition in the markets as well as general equilibrium effects.

From the labor market perspective, off-shoring induces cost savings and facilitates an increase in the firm's market share globally and competitiveness. Off-shoring also impacts on firm's technology and innovation as R & D offshoring impacts on productivity at home by reallocating market shares and allowing firms to sell more, and that firms achieve this goal by adapting products or services to local needs and charging lower prices. R & D offshoring alters the type of inputs and the nature of the task performed in the home country. Offshoring may serve to argument innovation at the multinational firm's home country by enabling the firm to benefit from the transfer of technology and knowledge from affiliates in the foreign country back home.

In view of these findings, firms are justified to relocate production to foreign countries to reduce production costs and gain access to foreign markets. Relocation to foreign markets may also be associated with the destruction in the domestic job; however, in general, the net effect is quite limited and is accompanied with task upgrading. The upgrading of the task requires firms to employ domestic workers that have the right skills. A negligible net effect could be concealing wage polarization and non-negligible polarization among domestic workers of varied skills. Therefore, policy challenge should be to facilitate domestic workers to seize and use the opportunity for job upgrading. This idea of facilitating domestic workers to seize and use the opportunity for job upgrade can be achieved by firms establishing the type of cognitive and communication skills that domestic enterprises find it hard to find abroad.

In addition, in view of the studies analyzed herein, off-shoring is a justifiable means to achieve competitive advantage. It can serve as a useful tool for a company to achieve productivity and cost-saving, and reorganization. No evidence exists to confirm the view that offshoring can be a threat to the economies of advanced countries or a threat to long-term competitiveness and innovative capacities of advanced countries. However, companies choosing to engage in offshoring needs to approach is with caution as there are risks being mitigated to achieve the positive impacts highlighted here.

As demonstrated in this book, off-shore outsourcing risks are reduced product quality, loss of control over suppliers, and undesirable consequences. From the supply chain business perspective, risks of offshore can be identified at phase 1 and phase 2 of the outsourcing process Risks at ex-ante contract phase occur during contract development, decision-making, and supplier selection stages of the outsourcing process. During this phase, notable risks are supply market environment risks, namely economic risks, cultural risks, and political risks. Others include political risks, environmental regulations and laws, unpredictable changes in labor, political instability, language and cultural barriers. Risks during the ex-post contract phase occur during supplier management stage of the offshore outsourcing process. These risks include experience risks; opportunistic behaviors and insufficient capability on the part of the supplier; firm's lack of experience in offshore outsourcing; risks of escalating costs linked to unexpected management costs and transactions; risks related to outsourcing expertise and experience and internal uncertainty in relation to outsourcing requirements, risks associated with supplier's opportunistic behaviors; and lack of capability; and unintentional knowledge leakage and conflicts. Company leaders must also be prepared to mitigate performance and relational risks when considering offshoring. Performance risk arises from a failure to achieve strategic objectives of partners by partners in an offshore outsourcing relationship despite there being cooperation. Performance risk includes factors related to performance that can lead to a reduction in the firm's performance or failure of a partnership. These factors include incomplete contractual specifications and the lack of capability on the part of the supplier.

The result of the analysis of studies on re-shoring also suggests that the critics of off-shoring may be wrong on drivers of re-shoring. In view of the findings analyzed herein, various factors influenced companies to reconsider their offshoring decisions in favor of re-shoring. Notable drivers of re-shoring include cost concerns; lack of internal competence; quality concerns; location factors (the growth of regional and local market (i.e., wage costs); human capital; the availability of resources; scientific infrastructure; and the presence of suppliers). Other location factors known to drive re-shoring include underestimation and miscalculation of full costs; production, innovation and co-location of R & D; off-shoring as a potential threat to intellectual property; balancing risk dispersion and costs savings;

proximity to the market to achieve flexibility; and the oil/shale gas resolution in the United States and a weakening dollar. For some companies, the intended consequences of off-shoring activities were not recognized. This and other factors appear to have led to the failure by companies to achieve the intended objectives of off-shoring and thus consider re-shoring production back to home countries or those closer to the parent countries.

In view of these findings, it is worth concluding that the re-shoring practices should be continued for reasons discussed herein. While various forms of trade barriers, notably legal, informational, and administrative barriers exist, off-shoring may be a worthy decision as it may be the most effective way to reach foreign customers. Relocating production abroad may also be an effective way to source from cheap foreign suppliers and thus cut costs. Companies can also capitalize on off-shoring to directly seek cheap labor abroad.

REFERENCES

Abraham, K. G., & Taylor, S. K. (1996). Firms' use of outside contractors: Theory and evidence, *Journal of Labour Economics, 14*, 394-424. doi:10.1086/209816

Acemoglu, D., & Autor, D. (2011). Skills, tasks, and technologies: Implications for employment and earnings. *Handbook of Labour Economics,* (4), 1043-1171). doi:10.1016/S0169-7218(11)02410-5

Acemoglu, D., Gancia, G., & Zilibotti, F. (2012). Off shoring and directed technical change. *National Bureau of Economic Research. Working Paper, no 18595, National Bureau of Economic Research.*

Afuah, A. (2001). Dynamic boundaries of the firm: are firms better off being vertically integrated in the face of a technological change? *Academy of Management Journal, 4*, 1211-1228. doi:10.2307/3069397

Agnese, P., & Ricart, J. E. (2009). Offshoring: Facts and figures at the country level. *IESE Research Papers D/792, IESE Business School.*

Albert, S., & Whetten, D. A. (1985). Organizational identity. *Research in Organizational Behaviour, 7*, 263–295.

Allen, T. D., Freeman, D. M., Russell, J. E., Reizestein, R. C., & Rentz, J. O. (2001). Survivor reactions to organizational downsizing: Does time ease the pain? *Journal of Occupational and Organizational Psychology, 74*(2), 145-164. doi:10.1348/096317901167299

Ambos, B., & Ambos, T. C. (2011). Meeting the challenge of offshoring R&D: An examination of firm-and location-specific factors. *R & D Management, 41*(2), 107–119. doi:10.1111/j.1467-9310.2010.00625.x

Amiti, M., & Konings, J. (2007). Trade liberalization, intermediate inputs, and productivity: Evidence from Indonesia. *American Economic Review, 97*, 1611-1638. doi:10.1257/aer.97.5.1611

Amiti, M., & Wei, S. 2006),'Service outsourcing, productivity and employment: Evidence from the US. *Discussion Paper, No. 5475, Centre for Economic Policy Research, London.*

Ancarani, A., Di Mauro, C., Fratocchi, L., Orzes, G., & Sartor, M. (2015). Prior to reshoring: A duration analysis of foreign manufacturing venture, *International Journal of Production Economics, 169*, 141-155. doi:10.1016/j.ijpe.2015.07.031

Ann, H., & McMillan, M. (2011). Offshoring Jobs? Multinationals and U.S. Manufacturing Employment. *The Review of Economics and Statistics, 93*, 857–75. doi:10.1162/REST_a_00085

Arlbjørn, J., & Mikkelsen, O. (2014). Backshoring manufacturing: notes on an important but under-researched theme, *Journal of Purchasing & Supply Management, 20*(1), 60-62. http://dx.doi.org/10.1016/j.pursup.2014.02.003

Aron, R., & Singh, J. (2005). Getting offshoring right. *Harvard Business Review, 83*, 135-147. Retrieved from http://hbr.org/2005/12/getting-offshoring-right/ar/1

Autor, D. H. (2003). Outsourcing at will: The contribution of unjust dismissal doctrine to the growth of employment outsourcing. *Journal of Labour Economics*, 1-42. https://dx.doi.org/10.1086/344122

Autor, D., Dorn, D., & Hanson, G. (2013). The China syndrome: Local labour market effects of import competition in the United States, *American Economic Review, 103*, 2121–2168. http://dx.doi.org/10.1257/aer.103.6.2121

Autor, D., Katz, L. F., & Kearney, M. S. (2008). Trends in U.S. wage inequality: Revising the revisionists. *The Review of Economics and Statistics, 90*, 300–323. doi:10.1162/rest.90.2.300

Baily, M. N., & Bosworth, B. P. (2014). U.S. manufacturing: Understanding its past and its potential future. *Journal of Economic Perspectives, 28*(1), 3-26. doi:10.1257/jep.28.1.3

Balakrishnan, S., & Wernerfelt, B. (1986). Technical change, competition, and vertical integration. *Strategic Management Journal*, 7, 347-359. doi:10.1002/smj.4250070405

Baldwin, J. R., & Gu, W. (2008). Outsourcing and offshoring in

Canada. *Statistics Canada Economic Analysis (EA),* Research Paper Series No. 055. Retrieved from https://www150.statcan.gc.ca/n1/pub/11f0027m/11f0027m2008055-eng.pdf

Bals, L., Jensen, P. D. Ø., Larsen, M. M., & Pedersen, T. (2013). Exploring layers of complexity in offshoring research and practice. In T. Pedersen, L. Bals, P. D. Ørberg Jensen, & M. Møller Larsen (Eds.), *The offshoring challenge: Strategic design and innovation for tomorrow's organization*, 1–18. London, UK: Springer.

Bals, L., Kirchoff, J. F., & Foerstl, K. (2016). Exploring the re-shoring and insourcing decision-making process: Toward an agenda for future research. *Operation Management.*, *9*(3), 102–116. doi:10.1007/s12063-016-0113-0

Bandura, A. (1997). *Self-efficacy: The exercise of control.* New York, NY: W. H. Freeman.

Barba Navaretti, G., & Falzoni, A. M. (2004). Home country effects of foreign direct investment. In G. Barba Navaretti, & A. J. Venables (Eds.), *Multinational firms in the world economy* (pp. 217-239). Princeton, NJ: Princeton University Press,

Barba Navaretti, G. B., Castellani, D., & Disdier, A. C. (2010). How does investing in cheap labour countries affect performance at home? Firm-level evidence from France and Italy. *Oxford Economic Papers*, *62*(2), 234–260. doi:10.1093/oep/pgp010

Barkema, H. G., Shenkar, O., Vermeulen, F., & Bell, J. H. J. (1997). Working abroad, working with others: How firms learn to operate international joint ventures. *Academy of Management Journal*, *40*, 426-442. doi:10.2307/256889

Barnard, H. (2010). Overcoming the liability of foreignness without strong firm capabilities: The value of market-based resources. *Journal of International Management*, *16*(2), 165-176. doi:10.1016/j.intman.2010.03.007

Bartel, A. P., Lach, S., & Sicherman, N. (2005). Outsourcing and technological change. *Centre for Economic Policy Research, Discussion Paper No. 5082.* doi:10.3386/w11158

Barthelemy, J. (2003). The seven deadly sins of outsourcing. *Academy of Management Executive*, *17*(2), 87-98. doi:10.5465/AME.2003.10025203

Batt, R., & Hiro N. (2009). How institutions and business strategies affect wages: A cross national study of call centers. *Industrial and Labour Relations Review, 62*, 533–552. doi:10.1177/001979390906200404

Baumgarten, D., Geishecker, I., & H. Görg, H. (2013). Offshoring, tasks, and the skill-wage pattern. *European Economic Review, 61*(3), 132–152. doi:10.1016/j.euroecorev.2013.03.007

Baumol, W. (2002). *The free-market innovation machine: Analyzing the growth miracle of capitalism.* Princeton, NJ: Princeton University Press.

Becker, S. O., Ekholm, K., & Muendler, M. A. (2013). Offshoring and the onshore composition of tasks and skills. *Journal of International Economics, 90*, 91–106. doi:10.1016/j.jinteco.2012.10.005

Belderbos R. (2003). Entry mode, organizational learning, and R & D in foreign affiliates: Evidence from Japanese firms. *Strategic Management Journal, 24*(3), 235–259. doi:10.1002/smj.294

Benito, G. R. (2015). Why and how motives (still) matter. *The Multinational Business Review, 23*(1), 15-24. doi:10.1108/MBR-02-2015-0005

Berlingieri, G. (2013). Outsourcing and the rise in services, *CEP Discussion Papers dp1199.* Centre for Economic Performance, LSE. Retrieved from http://cep.lse.ac.uk/pubs/download/dp1199.pdf

Bernard, A. B., Fort, T.C., Smeets, V., & Warzynski, F. (2018). Off-shoring and reorganization. *Working Paper.* Retrieved from http://faculty.tuck.dartmouth.edu/images/uploads/faculty/andrew-bernard/BFSW_Offshoring_Reorg_latest.pdf

Bierly, P., Damanpour, F., & Santoro, M. D. (2009). The application of external knowledge: organizational conditions for exploration and exploitation. *Journal of Management Studies, 46*, 481–509. doi:10.1111/j.1467-6486.2009.00829.x

Blinder, A. S. (2009). How many U.S. jobs might be offshorable? *World Economics, 10*(2), 41–78. Retrieved from https://www.princeton.edu/~ceps/workingpapers/142blinder.pdf

Bloom, N., Sadun, R., & Van Reenen, J. (2005). It ain't what you do, It's the way you do it: Testing explanations of productivity growth using U.S. affiliates. Retrieved from http://www.statistics.gov.uk/articles/nojournal/sadun_bvr25.pdf

Bogar, M. A., & Holmes, M. D. (2013). *Made in Mexico, An increasingly viable alternative to Chinese outsourcing*. Boston, MA: The Boston Company.

Boler, E. A., Moxnes, A., & Ulltveit-Moe, K. H. (2015). R & D, International sourcing and the joint impact on firm performance. *American Economic Review, 105*, 3704-3739. doi:10.1257/aer.20121530

Borzo, J. (2004). Scattering the seeds of invention: The globalization of research and development. New York, NY: *The Economist Intelligence Unit.*

Bottini, N., Ernst, C., & Luebker, M. (2011). *Economic and labour market paper 2007 11 offshoring and the labour market: What are the issues?* Retrieved from http://ilo.org/wcmsp5/groups/public/---ed_emp/---emp_elm/---analysis/documents/publication/wcms_113922.pdf

Bowlby, J. (1969). *Attachment and loss: Attachment.* New York, NY: Basic Books.

Brouthers, K. D., Lance, E., B., & Steve, W. (2008). Real options, international entry mode choice and performance. *Journal of Management Studies, 45*, 936-960.

Brown, D., & Wilson, S. (2005). *The Black Book of outsourcing: How to manage the changes, challenges, and opportunities.* Hoboken, NJ: Wiley & Sons.

Buckley, P. J. (2011). International integration and coordination in the global factory. *Management International Review, 51*, 269-283. doi:10.1007/s11575-011-0075-2

Bunyaratavej, K., Hahn, E. D., & Doh, J. P. (2007). International offshoring of services: A parity study. *Journal of International Management, 13*(1), 7-21. doi:10.1016/j.intman.2006.05.002

Byrne, Z. S., & Cropanzano, R. (2001). History of organizational justice: The founders speak. In R. Cropanzano (Ed.), *Justice in the workplace. Vol. II: From theory to practice.* Mahwah, NJ: Lawrence Erlbaum.

Cabral, S., Quelin, B., & Maia, W. (2013). Outsourcing failure and reintegration: the influence of contractual and external factors. *Long Range Planning, 47*(6), 1-14. doi:10.1016/j.lrp.2013.08.005

Calderini, M., & Scellato, G. (2005). Academic research, technological specialization, and the innovation performance in European regions: An empirical analysis in the wireless sector. *Industrial & Corporate Change, 142*, 279-305. doi:10.1093/icc/dth054

Cantwell, J., & Piscitello, L. (2007). Attraction and deterrence in the location of foreign/owned R & D activities: The role of positive and negative spill overs. *International Journal of Technological Learning, Innovation and Development, 1*(1), 83-111. doi:10.1504/IJTLID.2007.015020

Cantwell, J., & Santangelo, G. D. (19990. The frontier of international technology networks: sourcing abroad the most highly tacit capabilities. *Information Economics and Policy, 11*(1), 101-123. doi:10.1016/S0167-6245(99)00005-0

Carbone, V., & Moatti, V. (2016). The missing links in offshoring and backshoring research: learning through the 6 foundational premises of the theory of the supply chain. *Supply Chain Forum: An International Journal, 17*(4), 183-189. doi:10.1080/16258312.2016.1250475

Casson, M. (2013). *The growth of international business (RLE International Business)*. Oxon, Oxfordshire: Routledge.

Castellani, D., & Pieri, F. (2013). R & D offshoring and the productivity growth of European regions. *Research Policy, 42*, 1581–1594. doi:10.1016/j.respol.2013.05.009

Castellani, D., & Pieri, F. (2014). R & D Offshoring and the productivity growth of European regions, 74-300. *Comprehensive research papers on Global Innovation Networks: Challenges and opportunities for policy.* Retrieved from http://www.feemdeveloper.net/UserFiles/INGINEUS_D10.1_part2.pdf

Castellani, D., & Zanfei, A. (2006). *Multinational firms, innovation, and productivity.* Cheltenham, Gloucestershire, UK: Edward Elgar.

Cauto, V., Mani, M., Lewin, A., & Peeters, C. (2006). The globalization of white-collar work. *Duke Offshoring Network.* Retrieved from http://www.cedma-europe.org/newsletter%20articles/misc/The%20Globalization%20of%20White%20Collar%20Work%20(Oct%2006).pdf

Cavusgil, S. T., Yaprak, A., & Yeoh, P. (1993). A decision-making framework for global sourcing. *International Business Review, 2*(2), 143-156. doi:10.1016/0969-5931(93)90011-K

Chandler, A. D. (1990). *Scale and scope: The dynamics of capitalism*. Cambridge, MA: Harvard University Press.

Chapman, R., & Corso, M. (2005). From continuous improvement to collaborative innovation: The next challenge in supply chain management. *Production Planning & Control, 16*, 339-344. doi:10.1080/09537280500063269

Ciarli, T., Leoncini, R., Montresor, S., & Valente, M. (2008). Technological change and the vertical organization of industries. *Journal of Evolutionary Economics, 18*, 367-387. doi:10.1007/s00191-008-0092-x

Clever Age. (2006). Offshoring / back-shoring. Retrieved from http://www.clever-age.com/veille/clever-link/offshoring-backshoring-l-art-de-tourner-en-rond

Click, R., & Duening, T. (2005). *Business process outsourcing the competitive advantage*. Hoboken, NJ: Wiley & Sons.

Contractor, F. J., Kumar, V., Kundu, S. K., & Pedersen, T. (2010). Reconceptualizing the firm in a world of outsourcing and offshoring: The organizational and geographical relocation of high-value company functions. *Journal of Management Studies, 47*, 1417-1433. doi:10.1111/j.1467-6486.2010.00945.x

Costa, C. (2001). Information technology outsourcing in Australia: A literature review. *Information Management and Computer Security, 9*(5), 213-224. doi:10.1108/EUM0000000006068

Costinot, A., & Vogel, J. (2010). Matching and inequality in the world economy. *Journal of Political Economy, 118*, 747–786. doi:10.3386/w14672

Coyle-Shapiro, J. A. M., & Kessler, I. (2002). Exploring reciprocity through the lens of the psychological contract: Employee and employer perspectives. *European Journal of Work and Organizational Psychology, 11*(1), 69–86. doi:10.1080/13594320143000852

Crino, R. (2009). Offshoring, multinationals, and labour market: A review of the empirical literature. *Journal of Economic Surveys, 23*(2), 197-249. doi:10.1111/j.1467-6419.2008.00561.x

Cuervo-Cazurra, A. (2006). Who cares about corruption? *Journal of*

International Business Studies, 37, 807–822. doi:10.1057/palgrave.jibs.8400223

David, H., Jørgensen, R., Munch, J., &Xiang, C. (2014). The wage effects of offshoring: Evidence from Danish Matched Worker-Firm Data. *The American Economic Review*. American Economic Association. doi:10.2307/42920860

D'Agostino, L. M., Laursen, K.., & Santangelo, G. D. (2013). The impact of R & D offshoring on the home knowledge production of OECD investing regions. *Journal of Economic Geography, 13*, 145-175. doi:10.1093/jeg/lbs012

Dachs, B., & Zanker C. (2015). Backshoring of production activities in European manufacturing MPRA. Paper No. 63868. Retrieved from http://mpra.ub.uni-muenchen.de/63868/

Dachs, B., Ebersberger, B., Kinkel, S., & Som, O. (2014). The Effects of production offshoring on R & D and innovation in the home country. *Fraunhofer ISI Discussion Papers Innovation Systems and Policy Analysis No. 39*. doi:10.1007/s40812-014-0001-2

Dunning, J. H. (1988). The eclectic paradigm of international production: A restatement and some possible extensions. *Journal of International Business Studies, 19*, 1-31. doi:10.1007/978-1-137-54471-1_3

Das, T. K., & Teng, B. (1996). Risk types and inter-firm alliance structures. *Journal of Management Studies, 33*, 827-843. doi:10.1111/j.1467-6486.1996.tb00174.x

Demirbag, M., Mellahi, S., Sahadev, K., & Elliston, J. (2012). Employee service abandonment in service operations: A case study of a US multinational in India. *Journal of World Business, 47*(2), 178-185. doi:10.1016/j.jwb.2011.04.004

Deardorff, A. V. (2001). Fragmentation in simple trade models. *North American Journal of Economics and Finance, 12*(2), 121-137. doi:10.1016/S1062-9408(01)00043-2

Desai, M. A., Fritz Foley, C., &, Hines, J. R. (2009). Domestic effects of the foreign activities of U.S. multinationals. *American Economic Journal: Economic Policy, 1*(1),181–203. doi:10.1257/pol.1.1.181

Desai, M. A., Foley, C., & Hines, J. R. (2009). Domestic effects of the foreign activities of U.S. multinationals. *American Economic Journal of Economic Policy, 1*(1), 181-203. doi:10.1257/pol.1.1.181

Dey, M., Houseman, S., & Polivka, A. (2010). What do we know about contracting out in the United States? Evidence from household and establishment surveys in labour in the new economy. *National Bureau of Economic Research*. Retrieved from http://ideas.repec.org/h/nbr/nberch/10824.html

Dhar, S., & Balakrishnan, B. (2006). Risks, benefits, and challenges in global IT outsourcing: Perspectives and practices. *Journal of Global Information Management, 14*(3), 59-89. doi:10.4018/jgim.2006070104

Di Gregorio, D., Musteen, M., & Thomas, D. E. (2009). Offshore outsourcing as a source of international competitiveness for SMEs. *Journal of International Business Studies, 40*, 969-988. doi:10.1057/jibs.2008.90

Dibbern, J., Winkler, J., & Heinzl, A. (2008). Explaining variations in client extra costs between software projects offshored to India. *MIS Quarterly, 32*(2), 333-366. doi:10.2307/25148843

Doh, P. (2005). Offshore outsourcing: Implications for international business and strategic management theory and practice, *Journal of Management Studies, 42*, 695–704. doi:10.1111/j.1467-6486.2005.00515.x

Dryer, J. H., & Singh, H. (1998). The relational view: Cooperative strategy and sources of inter-organizational competitive advantages. *The Academy of Management Review, 23*(660-679). doi:10.2307/259056

Dube, A., & Kaplan, E. (2010). Does outsourcing reduce wages in the low-wage service occupations? Evidence from janitors and guards, *Industrial and Labour Relations Review*, 287—306. doi:10.1177/001979391006300206

Duke University CIBER / Archstone Consulting. (2005). *First biannual offshoring survey results*. Retrieved from http://www.outsourcing-information-technology.com/university.html

Dunning, J. H. (1980). Toward an eclectic theory of international production: Some empirical tests. *Journal of International Business Standards, 11*(1), 9–31. doi:10.1007/978-1-137-54471-1

Dunning, J. H. (1998). Location and the multinational enterprise: A neglected factor? *Journal of International Business Studies, 29*(1), 45-66. doi:10.1057%2Fpalgrave.jibs.8490024.pdf

Earl, M. J. (1996). The risks of outsourcing IT. *Sloan Management Review, 37*(3), 26-32. doi:10.4236/ib.2013.53B036

Ebenstein A., Harrison, A. McMillan, M., & Phillips, S. (2014). Estimating the impact of trade and offshoring on American workers using the current population surveys. *The Review of Economics and Statistics, 96*, 581–595. doi:10.1162/REST_a_00400

Egger, H., & Egger, P. (2003). Outsourcing and skill-specific employment in a small economy: Austria after the fall of the Iron Curtain. *Oxford Economic Papers, 55*, 625-643. doi:10.1093/oep/55.4.625

Egger, H., Kreickemeier, U., & Wrona, J. (2015). Offshoring domestic jobs. *Journal of International Economics, 97*, 112-125. doi:10.1016/j.jinteco.2015.03.010

Egger, P., & Pfaffermayr, M. (2009). Multinationals have higher domestic investments than national firms. *Leverhulme Centre for Research on Globalisation and Economic Policy (GEP)*. Nottingham, England: University of Nottingham.

Egger, H., Kreickemeier, U., & Wrona, J. (2015). Offshoring domestic jobs. *Journal of International Economics, 97*(1), 112-125. doi:10.1016/j.jinteco.2015.03.010

Ehie, I. C. (2001). Determinants of success in manufacturing outsourcing decisions: A survey study. *Production and Inventory Management Journal, 42*(1), 31. Retrieved from http://orp.aiub.edu/WorkingPaper/WorkingPaper.aspx?year=2008

Elhaan, H., Melitz, M., & Yeaple, S. (2004). Exports versus FDI with heterogeneous firms. *American Economic Review, 94,* 300–316. doi:10.3386/w9439

Ellram, L. M., Tate, W. L., & Billington, C. (2008). Offshore outsourcing of professional services: A transaction cost economics perspective. *Journal of Operations Management, 26*(2), 148-163. doi:10.1016/j.jom.2007.02.008

Ellram, L. M., Tate, W. L., & Petersen, K. J. (2013). Offshoring and reshoring: An update on the manufacturing location decision. *Journal of Supply Chain Management, 49*, 14-22. doi:10.1111/jscm.12019

Eli, B., Bound, J., & Machin, S. (1998). Implications of Skill-Biased Technological Change: International Evidence. *The Quarterly Journal of Economics*. Oxford, England: Oxford University Press. doi:10.2307/2586980

Enderwick, P. (2008). Quality assurance and upgrading in global supply chains: Implications for management in a transition economy. *Thunderbird International Business Review, 50*(4), 217-230. doi:10.1002/tie.20200

Engardio, P. (2006). Outsourcing: Job killer or innovation boost? *Business Week.* Retrieved from https://www.bloomberg.com/news/articles/2006-11-08/businessweek

Ernst, D. (2010). Upgrading through innovation in a small network economy: insights from Taiwan's IT industry. *Economics of Innovation & New Technology, 19*(4), 295-324. doi:10.438590802469560

Farrell, D. (2003). *Offshoring: Is it a win-win game?* San Francisco, CA: McKinsey Global Institute.

Farrell, D. (2005). Offshoring: Value creation through economic change. *Journal of Management Studies, 42,* 675-683. doi:10.1111/j.1467-6486.2005.00513.x

Federico, S. (2014). Industry dynamics and competition from low-wage countries: Evidence on Italy. *Oxford Bulletin of Economics and Statistics, 76*, 389-410. doi:10.1111/obes.12023

Feeney, J., & Noller, P. (1996). *Adult attachment.* Thousand Oaks, CA: Sage.

Feenstra, R. C., & Jensen, J. B. (2012). Evaluating estimates of materials off shoring from U.S. manufacturing. *Economics Letters, 117*(1), 170-173. doi:10.3386/w17916

Feenstra, R. C. (2010). *Off shoring in the global economy: Microeconomic structure and macroeconomic implications.* Cambridge, MA: The MIT Press.

Feenstra, R. C. (2017). *Statistics to measure offshoring and its impact.* Cambridge, MA: National Bureau of Economic Research. doi:10.3386/w23067

Fifarek, B. J., Veloso, F. M., & Davidson, C. I. (2008). Offshoring technology innovation: A case study of rare-earth technology. *Journal of Operations Management, 26*(2), 222-238. doi:10.1016/j.jom.2007.02.013

Fineman, S. (2003). *Understanding emotions at work*. London, UK: Sage.

Foerstl, K., Kirchoff, J. F., & Bals, L. (2016). Reshoring and insourcing: drivers and future research directions, *International Journal of Physical Distribution and Logistics Management*, *46*, 492-515. doi:10.1108/IJPDLM-02-2015-0045

Foster-McGregor, N., Stehrer, R., & de Vries, G. (2013), Offshoring and the skill structure of labour demand. *Review of World Economics*, *149*, 631-662. doi:10.1007/s10290-013-0163-4

Fratocchi, L., Ancarani, A., Barbieri, P., Di Mauro, C., Nassimbeni, G., Sartor, M., Vignoli, M., & Zanoni, A. (2016). Motivations of manufacturing reshoring: An interpretative framework. *International Journal of Physics Distribution and Logistical Management, 46*(2), 98–127. doi:10.1108/IJPDLM-06-2014-0131

Fratocchi, L., Iapadre, L., Ancarani, A., Di Mauro, C., Zanoni, A., & Barbieri, P. (2014). Manufacturing reshoring: threat and opportunity for East Central Europe and Baltic Countries, In A. Zhuplev, (Ed.), *Geo-regional competitiveness in Central and Eastern Europe* (pp. 83-119). The Baltic Countries, and Russia, IGI Global.

Freeman, R. (2005). What really ails Europe (and America): The doubling of the global workforce. *The Globalist.* Retrieved from http://www.theglobalist.com

Fredriksson, A., & Jonsson, P. (2009). Assessing the consequences of low-cost sourcing in China. *International Journal of Physical Distribution & Logistics Management*, *39*(3), 227-249. doi:10.1111/roie.12187

Fritsch, U., & Görg, H. (2013). Outsourcing, offshoring and innovation: Evidence from firm level data for emerging economies. *Kiel Institute for the World Economy. Working Paper No. 1861*, Kiel. doi:10.1111/roie.12187

Frost T. (2001). The geographic sources of foreign subsidiaries' innovations. *Strategic Management Journal*, *22*(2), 101–123. doi:10.1002/1097-0266(200101)22:2<101

Geishecker, I., & Görg, H. (2008). Winners and losers: A micro-level analysis of international outsourcing and wages. *Canadian Journal of Economics*, *41*, 243-270. doi:10.1111/j.1365-2966.2008.00462.x

Gianmarco, O. I., Peri, G., &. Wright, G. C. (2013). Immigration, Offshoring, and American Jobs. *American Economic Review, 103*, 1925–1959. doi:10.1257/aer.103.5.1925

Greg, W. C. (2014). Revisiting the employment impact of off-shoring. *European Economic Review, 66*, 63–83. doi:10.1016/j.euroecorev.2013.11.008

Ghosh, I. (2018). Productive offshoring: Evidence from Spain. *Canadian Journal of Economics*, 1-48. doi:10.2139/ssrn.3298490

Ghosh, I. D. (2017). *Productive offshoring: evidence from Spain*. Retrieved from https://www.usitc.gov/publications/332/.../ecwp-2017-10-a-10-03-17-as-pdf.pdf

Ghoshal, S. (1987). Global strategy: An organizing framework. *Strategic Management Journal, 8,* 425-440. doi:10.1002/smj.4250080503

Gopal, A., Sivaramakrishnan, K., Krishnan, M. S., & Mukhopad-hyay, T. (2003). Contracts in offshore software development: An empirical analysis. *Management Science, 49*, 1671-1683. doi:10.1287/mnsc.49.12.1671.25120

Görg H. (2011). Globalization, off shoring and jobs. In M. Bacchetta, & M/ Jansen, (Ed.), *Making globalization socially sustainable. International Labour Organization (ILO) and World Trade Organization (WTO),* (pp. 21-47).

Görg, H., & Hanley, A. (2011). Services outsourcing and innovation: An empirical investigation. *Economic Inquiry, 49*, 321–333. doi:10.1111/j.1465-7295.2010.00299

Görg, H. Hanley, A., & Strobl, E. (2008). Productivity effects of international outsourcing: evidence from plant-level data. *Canadian Journal of Economics, 41*, 670–688. doi:10.1111/j.1540-5982.2008.00481.x

Gottfredson, M., Puryear, P., & Phillips S. (2005, February). Strategic sourcing: From periphery to the core. *Harvard Business Review*, 5, 132-139. Retrieved from https://www.ncbi.nlm.nih.gov/pubmed/15724581

Graf, M., & Mudambi S. M. (2005). The outsourcing of IT-enabled business processes: A conceptual model of the location decision. *Journal of International Management, 11*(2), 253-268. doi:10.1016/j.intman.2005.03.010

Grappi, S., Romani, S., & Bagozzi, R. P. (2015). Consumer responses to corporate offshoring practices. *Management Decision, 53*, 698-712. doi:10.1108/MD-09-2014-0552

Gray, J. V., Skowronsky, K., Esenduran, G., & Rungtudanatham, M.J. (2013). Reshoring phenomenon: what supply chain academics ought to know and should do. *Journal of Supply Chain Management, 49*(2), 27-33. doi:10.1111/jscm.12012

Groizard, J. L., Ranjan, P., & Rodriguez-Lopez, A. (2015), Trade costs and job flows: Evidence from establishment-level data. *Economic Inquiry, 53*(1), 173–204. doi:10.1111/ecin.12139

Grossman, G. E., & Rossi-Hansberg, E. (2006). Trading tasks: A simple theory of offshoring. *Princeton Center for Globalisation and Governance Working Paper.*

Grossman, G. M., & Rossi-Hansberg, E. (2008). Trading tasks: A simple theory of offshoring. *American Economic Review, 98*, 1978–1997. doi:10.3386/w12721

Gulbrandsen, B., Sandvik, K., & Haugland, S. (2009). Antecedents of vertical integration: transaction cost economics and resource-based explanations. *Journal of Purchasing & Supply Management, 15*(2), 89-102. doi:10.1016/j.pursup.2008.12.003

Gupta, U. G., & Gupta, A. (1992). Outsourcing the IS function: Is it necessary for your organization? *Information System Management, 9*(2), 44-50. doi:10.1080/10580539208906881

Gylling, M., Heikkilä, J., Jussila, K., & Saarinen, M. (2015). Making decisions on offshore outsourcing and backshoring: A case study in the bicycle industry, *International Journal of Production Economics, 162*, 92-100. doi:10.1016/j.ijpe.2015.01.006

Hagedoorn, J. (1993). Understanding the rationale of strategic technology partnering: Interorganizational modes of cooperation and sectorial differences. *Strategic Management Journal, 14*, 371-385. doi:10.1002/smj.4250140505

Hallier, J. (2000). Security abeyance: Coping with the erosion of job conditions and treatment. *British Journal of Management*, 11. doi:10.1111/1467-8551.00152

Halpern, L., Koren, M., & Szeidl, A. (2015). Imported inputs and productivity. *American Economic Review, 105*, 3660-3703. doi:10.1257/aer.2015443

Hameri, A. P., & Hintsa, J. (2009). Assessing the drivers of change for cross border supply chains. *International Journal of Physical Distribution & Logistics Management, 39*, 741-761. doi:10.1108/09600030911008184

Handley, S. M., & Benton Jr., W. C. (2013). The influence of task- and location-specific complexity on the control and coordination costs in global outsourcing relationships. *Journal of Operations Management, 31*(3), 109-128. doi:10.1016/j.jom.2012.12.003

Handley, S. M. (2012). The perilous effects of capability loss on outsourcing management and performance. *Journal of Operations Management, 30*(1), 152-165. doi:10.1016/j.jom.2011.10.003

Hansson, P. (2005). Skill upgrading and production transfer within Swedish multinationals. *Scandinavian Journal of Economics, 107*, 673-692. doi:10.1111/j.1467-9442.2005.00428.x

Haried, P., & Ramamurthy, K. (2009). Evaluating the success in international sourcing of information technology projects: The need for a relational client-vendor approach. *Project Management Journal, 40*(3), 56-71. doi:10.1002/pmj.20113

Harmon, P. (2003). *Business process change: A manager's guide to improving, redesigning, and automatic processes.* San Francisco, CA: Morgan Kaufmann Publishers.

Harrison, A., & McMillan, M. (2010). Offshoring Jobs? Multinationals and U.S. manufacturing employment. *Review of Economics and Statistics, 93*, 857-875. doi:10.1162/REST_a_00085

Hätönen, J. (2009). Making the locational choice: A case approach to the development of a theory of offshore outsourcing and internationalization. *Journal of International Management, 15*(1), 61-76. doi:10.1016/j.intman.2008.06.003

Head, K., & Ries, J. (2002). Offshore production and skill upgrading by Japanese manufacturing firms. *Journal of International Economics, 58*, 81-105. doi:10.1016/S0022-1996(01)00161-1

Helpman, E. (2006). Trade, FDI, and the organisation of firms. *Journal of Economic Literature XLIV*, 589-631. doi:10.3386/w12091

Helpman, E., Melitz, M. J., & Yeaple, S. R. (2004). Export versus FDI with heterogeneous firms. *American Economic Review, 94*(1), 300-316. doi:10.1257/000282804322970814

Henisz, W. J. (2000). The institutional environment for multinational investment. *Journal of Law, Economics and Organization, 16*(2), 334-364. doi:10.1093/jleo/16.2.334

Herath, T., & Kishore, R. (2009). Offshore outsourcing: Risks, challenges, and potential solutions. *Information Systems Management, 26*(4), 312-326. doi:10.1080/10580530903245549

Hijzen, A., & Swaim, P. (2007). Does offshoring reduce industry employment? *National Institute Economic Review, 201*(1), 86–96. doi:10.1177/0027950107083053

Hijzen, A., Inui, T., & Todo, Y. (2008). Does offshoring pay?: Firm-level evidence from Japan. *Economic Inquiry. Western Economic Association International, 48*, 880-895. doi:10.1111/j.1465-7295.2008.00175.x

Hira, R., & Hira, A. (2005). *Outsourcing America: What's behind our national crisis and how can we reclaim American jobs.* New York, NY: AMACOM.

Hirschfeld, R. R., & Field, H. S. (2000). Work centrality and work alienation: Distinct aspects of a general commitment to work. *Journal of Organizational Behaviour, 21*, 789–800. doi:10.1002/1099-1379(200011)21:73.0.CO;2-W

Hitt, M. A. Keats, B. W., & DeMarie, S. M. (1998). Navigating in the new competitive landscape: Building strategic flexibility and competitive advantage in the 21st century. *Academy of Management Executive, 12*(4), 22-42. doi:10.5465/ame.1998.1333922

Holz, R. (2009). *An investigation into O=off-Shoring and back-shoring in the German automotive industry* (Doctoral dissertation). University of Wales, Swansea.

Honess, S. (2003). Business process outsourcing. In J. Angel (Ed.), *Technology outsourcing* (pp. 208-229). London, UK: The New Society.

Horvit, M. (2004). Delphi among firms sending engineering: Research work out of U.S. *Fort Worth Star-Telegram.*

Howells, J. (1996). Tacit knowledge, innovation, and technology transfer. *Technology Analysis and Strategic Management, 8,* 91-106. doi:10.1080/09537329608524237

Hummels, D., Jørgenson, R., Munch, J., & Xiang, C. (2011). The age effects of outsourcing: Evidence from Danish matched worker-firm data. *NBER Working Paper No.17496.*

Hummels, D., Jrgensen, R., Munch, J. R., & Xiang, C. (2014). The wage effects of offshoring: Evidence from Danish matched worker-firm Data. *American Economic Review, 104*, 1597-1629. doi:10.1257/aer.104.6.1597

Industry Week. (2012). 7 key factors driving the offshoring of services. Retrieved from https://www.industryweek.com/global-economy/public-policy?page=135

Itami, H., & Thomas, R. (1987). *Mobilizing invisible assets.* Cambridge, MA: Harvard University Press.

Javalgi, R. G., Joseph, W. B., Granot, E., & Gross, A. C. (2013). Strategies for sustaining the edge in offshore outsourcing of services: The case of India. *Journal of Business & Industrial Marketing, 28*, 475–486. doi:10.1108/JBIM-04-2013-0103

Joubioux, C., & Vanpoucke, E. (2016). Towards right-shoring: a framework for off-and re-shoring decision-making, *Operation Management Review.* http://dx.doi.org/10.1007/s12063-016-0115-y

Kahn, W. A. (1998). Relational systems at work. *Research in Organizational Behaviour, 20*, 39–76. doi:10.5465/amr.2011.0363

Kakabadse, A., & Kakabadse, N. (2005). Outsourcing: Current and future. *Thunderbird International Business Review, 47*(2),183-204. doi:10.1002/tie.20048

Karpaty, P., & Tingvall, P. G. (2011). Offshoring and home country R & D. *CESIS Working Paper No. 254*, Stockholm.

Kasahara, H., & Rodrigue, J. (2008). Does the use of imported intermediates increase productivity? Plant-level evidence. *Journal of Development Economics, 87*(1), 106-118. doi:10.1016/j.jdeveco.2007.12.008

Katz, L. F., & Krueger, A. B. (2016). The Rise and nature of alternative work arrangements in the United States, 1995-2015. *NBER Working Paper No. 22667.*

Kedia, B. L., & Mukherjee, D. (2009). Understanding offshoring: A research framework based on disintegration, location and externalization advantages. *Journal of World Business, 44*, 250–261. doi:10.1016/j.jwb.2008.08.005

Keen, P. (1997). *The process edge-creating value where it counts.* Boston, MA: Harvard Business School Press.

Ketokivi, M., & Ali-Yrkkö, J. (2009). Unbundling R & D and manufacturing: post-industrial myth or economic reality? *Review of Policy Research, 26*, 35-54. doi:10.1111/j.1541-1338.2008.00368.x

Kinkel, S., & Maloca, S. (2009). Drivers and antecedents of manufacturing offshoring and backshoring: A German perspective. *Journal of Purchasing & Supply Management, 15*(3), 154-165. doi:10.1016/j.pursup.2009.05.007

Kinkel, S. (2012). Trends in production relocation and backshoring activities, *International Journal of Operations & Production Management, 32*, 696-720. doi:10.1108/01443571211230934

Kinnunen, U., Mauno, S., Nätti, J., & Happonen, M. (2000). Organizational antecedents and outcomes of job insecurity: A longitudinal study in three organizations in Finland. *Journal of Organizational Behaviour, 21*, 443-459. doi:10.1002/(SICI)1099-1379(200006)21:43.3.CO;2-E

Klein, B., Crawford, R., & Alchian, A. (1987). Vertical integration, appropriate rents and the competitive contracting process. *Journal of Law and Economics, 21,* 297-326. doi:10.1086/466922

Klein, H. J., Becker, T. E., & Meyer, J. P. (2009). *Commitment in organizations (SIOP Organizational Frontiers Series).* New York, NY: Routledge.

Klier, K. (2015). The growing importance of Mexico in North America's auto production, *Chicago Fed Letter.* The Federal Reserve Bank of Chicago, May 2013, Number 310.

Kohler, W. (2004). International outsourcing and factor prices with multistage production. *The Economic Journal, 114,* .C166-C185. doi:10.1111/j.0013-0133.2003.00204.x

Kogut B., & Zander, U. (1993). Knowledge of the firm and the evolutionary theory of the multinational corporation. *Journal of International Business Studies*, 625-645. doi:10.1057/palgrave.jibs.8400058

Kogut, B., & Kulatilaka, N. (2004). Real options pricing and organizations: The contingent risks of extended theoretical domains. *Academy of Management Review, 29*(1), 102-110. doi:10.5465/amr.2004.11851725

Kohlbacher, M., & Reijers, H. (2013). The effect of process-oriented organizational design on firm performance. *Business Process Management Journal, 19*(2), 245-262. doi:10.1108/14637151311308303

Kohler, W. K., & Smolka. M (2011). Sourcing premia with incomplete contracts: Theory and evidence. *Journal of Economic Analysis and Policy, 11*(1), art 10. doi:10.2202/1935-1682.2498

Kotabe, M. (19980. Efficiency vs effectiveness orientation of global sourcing strategy: A comparison of U.S. and Japanese multinational companies. *Academy of Management Executive, 12,* 107-119. doi:10.5465/AME.1998.1334000

Kotabe, M., & Murray, J. (2004). Global sourcing strategy and sustainable competitive advantage. *Industrial Marketing Management,* 33(1). 7-14. Doi;10.1016/j.indmarman.2003.08.004.

Kovak, B., Oldenski, L., & Sly, N. (2017). The labour market effects of offshoring by U.S. multinational firms: Evidence from changes in Global Tax Policy, *NBER working paper 23947*. doi:10.3386/w23947

Kuemmerle, W. (1999). The drivers of foreign direct investment into research and development: an empirical investigation. *Journal of International Business Studies, 301*, 1-24. Retrieved from http://www.palgrave-journals.com/jibs/journal/v30/n1/pdf/8490058a.pdf

Kurz, C. J. (2006). Outstanding outsourcers: A firm-and plant-level analysis of production sharing. *Federal Reserve Board Finance and Economics Discussion Series Paper No. 2006-04.*

Lacity, M. C., Iyer, V. V., & Rudramuniyaiah, P. S. (2008). Turnover intentions of Indian IS professionals. *Information Systems Frontiers, 10*(2), 225-241. doi:10.1007/978-3-540-88851-2_18

Lasi H., Fettke, P., Kemper H. G., Feld T., & Hoffmann, M. (2014). Industry 4.0. *Business and Information Systems Engineering, 6*(4), 239-242. doi:10.1007/s12599-014-0334-4

Leiblein, M., Reuer, J., & Dalsace, F. (2002). Do make or buy decisions matter?: The influence of organizational governance on technological performance. *Strategic Management Journal, 23*, 817–833. doi:10.1002/smj.259

Lewin, A. Y., & Couto, V. (2007). *Next generation offshoring: The globalization of innovation.* Raleigh, NC: Duke University, The Fuqua School of Business.

Lewin, A. Y., Massini, S., & Peeters, C. (2009). Why are companies offshoring innovation?: The emerging global race for talent. *Journal of International Business Studies, 40*, 901-925. doi:10.1057/jibs.2008.92

Lewin, A., & Peeters C. (2006). The top-line allure of offshoring. *Harvard Business Review, 84*, 22-24. Retrieved from https://hbr.org/2006/03/the-top-line-allure-of-offshoring

Lieb, R. C., & Lieb, K. J. (2009). *Penske Logistics Presents 3 PL CEO Survey Executive Summary.* Retrieved from http://www.gopenske.com/newsroom/2009_9_21_executive_summary.html

Lindič, J., & Marques da Silva, C. (2011). Value proposition as a catalyst for a customer focused innovation. *Management Decision, 49*, 1694-1708. doi:10.1108/00251741111183834

Loh, L., & Venkatraman, N. (1992). Determinants of information technology outsourcing: A cross-sectional analysis. *Journal of Management Information Systems, 9*(1), 7-24. doi:10.1080/07421222.1992.11517945

Mahnke, V., Lucas, M., & Vang, J. (2005). Strategic outsourcing of IT services: Theoretical stocktaking and empirical challenges. *Industry and Innovation, 12*(2), 205-253.doi:10.1080/13662710500087958

Manning, S. (2014). Mitigate, tolerate or relocate?: Offshoring challenges, strategic imperatives, and resource constraints, *Journal of World Business, 49*, 522-535. doi:10.1016/j.jwb.2013.12.006

Manning, S., Massini, S., & Lewin, C. (2008). A dynamic perspective on next-generation offshoring: the global sourcing of science and engineering talent. *Academy of Management Perspectives*, 35-54. doi:10.5465/AMP.2008.34587994

Manuj, I., & Mentzer, J. T. (2008). Global supply chain risk management strategies. *International Journal of Physical Distribution & Logistics Management, 38*(3), 192-223. doi:10.1108/09600030810866986

Markusen, J. R. (2002). *Multinational firms and the theory of international trade.* Cambridge, MA: MIT Press.

Martínez-Mora, C., & Merino, F. (2014). Offshoring in the Spanish footwear industry: A return journey? *Journal of Purchasing, Supply Management., 20,* 225–237.

Maskell, P., Pedersen, T., Petersen, B., & Dick-Nielsen, J. (2007). Learning paths to offshore outsourcing: From cost reduction to knowledge seeking. *Industry & Innovation, 143,* 239- 257. doi:10.2139/ssrn.982122

Mattarelli, W., & Tagliaventi, M. R. (2012). How offshore professionals' job dissatisfaction can promote further offshoring: Organizational outcomes of job crafting. *Journal of Management Studies,* Early view. doi:10.1111/j.1467-6486.2012.01088.x

Mayer, K. J., & Salomon, R. M. (2006). Capabilities, contractual hazards, and governance: Integrating resource-based and transaction cost perspectives. *Academy of Management Journal, 49,* 942-959. Retrieved from https://pdfs.semanticscholar.org/f58d/aaf1f386a0a64bc8941357de9ff5a68f2b52.pdf

Mazzanti, M., Montresor, S., & Pini, P. (2009). What drives (or hampers) outsourcing?: Evidence for a local production system in Emilia Romagna. *Industry and Innovation, 16,* 331-365. doi:10.1080/13662710902923909

McAllister, D. J. (1995). Affect-and cognition-based trust as foundations for interpersonal cooperation in organizations. *Academy of Management Journal, 38*(1), 24-59. doi:10.2307/256727

McIvor, R. (2009). How the transaction cost and resource-based theories of the firm inform outsourcing evaluation. *Journal of Operations Management, 27,* 45-63. doi 10.1016/j.jom.2008.03.004

Mehta, A., Armenakis, A., Mehta, N., & Irani, F. (2006). Challenges and opportunities of business process outsourcing in India. *Journal of Labour Research, 27*(3), 323-338. doi:10.1007/s12122-006-1026-8

Metiu, A. (2006). Owning the code: Status closure in distributed groups. *Organization Science, 17,* 418–435. doi:10.1287/orsc.1060.0195

Mihalache, O. R., Jansen, J. P., Van Den Bosch, F. A., & Volberda, H. W. (2012). Offshoring and firm innovation: The moderating role of top management team attributes. *Strategic Management Journal, 33*, 1480-1498. doi:10.1002/smj.1983

Milberg, W., & Winkler, D. (2010). Economic insecurity in the new wave of globalization: Offshoring and the labour share under varieties of capitalism. *International Review of Applied Economics, 24*, 285-308. doi:10.1080/02692171003701479

Michel, B., & Rycx, F. (2014). Productivity gains and spill overs from offshoring. *Review of International Economics, 22*(1), 73-85. doi:10.1111/roie.12097

Mills, J., Schmitz, J., & Frizelle, G. (2004). A strategic review of "supply networks." *International Journal of Operations & Production Management, 24*, 1012-1036. doi:10.1108/01443570410558058

Mitra, D., & Ranjan, P. (2010). Offshoring and unemployment: The role of search frictions labour mobility. *Journal of International Economics, 81*(2), 219–229. doi:10.1016/j.jinteco.2010.04.001

Mol, M., van Tulder R. J. M., & Beije, P. R. (2005). Antecedents and performance consequences of international outsourcing. *International Business Review, 14*, 599-617. doi:10.1016/j.ibusrev.2005.05.004

Morgan, S. J. (2009). *The human side of outsourcing: Psychological theory and management practice.* Oxford, UK: Wiley-Blackwell.

Moreno-Brid, J., & Santamaria, J. (2005). Industrialization and Economic Growth in Mexico after NAFTA: The Road Travelled. *Development and Cultural Change, 36*, 1095-1119. doi:10.1111/j.0012-155X.2005.00451.x

Morgan, S. J., & Symon, G. (2006). The experience of outsourcing transfer: Implications for guidance and counselling. *British Journal of Guidance and Counselling, 34*(2), 191–207. doi:10.1080/03069880600583238

Moser, C., & Zurich, E. (2010). Offshoring, firm performance, and establishment-level employment–identifying productivity and downsizing effects. *CEPR Discussion Paper No. DP7455.*

Mudambi, R. (2008). Location, control and innovation in knowledge-intensive industries. *Journal of Economic Geography, 8*, 699–725. doi:10.1093/jeg/lbn024

Nager, A., & Atkinson, R. D. (2015). The myth of America's manufacturing renaissance: *The real sate of U.S. manufacturing, the information*

Technology and Innovation Foundation. Retrieved from http://www2.itif.org/2015-myth-american-manufacturing-renaissance.pdf

Naghavi, A., & Ottaviano, G. (2009). Offshoring and product innovation. *Economic Theory, 38*, 517-532. doi:10.1007/s00199-007-0322-8

Narula R., & Zanfei, A. (2005). Globalisation of Innovation. In J. Fagerberg, D. Mowery, & R. R. Nelson (Eds.), *Handbook of innovation* (pp. 318–345). Oxford, UK: Oxford University Press.

Narula, R., &. Michel, J. (2009). Reverse knowledge transfer and its implications for European policy. *Maastricht: UNU-MERIT Working Paper.*

NASSCOM. (2010). The IT-BPO Sector in India–Nasscom. *NASSCOM-* Strategic Review 2010. Retrieved from http://www.nasscom.org

NASSCOM. (2009). The IT-BPO Sector in India-Strategic Review 2009. Retrieved from http://www.nasscom.org

Neureiter, M., & Nunnenkamp, P. (2010). Outsourcing motives, location choice, and labour market implications: An empirical analysis for European Countries. *Kyklos, 63*, 206-230. doi:10.1111/j.1467-6435.2010.00470.x

Nieto, M. J., & Rodríguez, A. (2011). Offshoring of R & D: Looking abroad to improve innovation performance. *Journal of International Business Studies, 42*, 345–361. doi:10.1057/jibs.2010.59

Norwood, J., Carson, C., Deese, N., Johnson, F, Reader, J., & Schwab, S. (2006). Off-shoring: An elusive phenomenon. *National Academy of Public Administration.* A Report of the Panel of the National Academy of Public Administration for the U.S. Congress and the Bureau of Economic Analysis.

Nordin, F., & Henrik, A. (2008). Business service sourcing: A literature review and agenda for future research. *International Journal of Integrated Supply Management,* (4), 378-405. doi:10.1504/IJISM.2008.020760

Olsen, K. B. (2006). Productivity impacts of offshoring and outsourcing: A review. *OECD Science, Technology and Industry Working Paper No. 2006/*1.

Ottaviano, G., Peri, G., & Wright, G. (2013). Immigration, offshoring, and American jobs. *American Economic Review, 103*, 1925–1959. doi:10.1257/aer.103.5.1925

Outsource Portfolio Blog. (2010). Retrieved from http://outsourceportfolio.com/

Ozawa, T. (2008). History repeats itself: Evolutionary structural change and TNC's involvement in infrastructure overseas, flying Geese Style, Working Paper 261. Columbia: *Centre on Japanese Economy and Business, Columbia Business School.*

Palugod, N. (2011). Global trends in offshoring and outsourcing. *International Journal of Business and Social Science, 2*(16), 11-19. Retrieved from http://ijbssnet.com/journals/Vol_2_No_16_September_2011/2.pdf

Parmigiani, A. E. (2007). Why do firms both make and buy?: An investigation of concurrent sourcing. *Strategic Management Journal, 28*, 285-311. doi:10.1002/smj.580

Parteka, A., & Wolszczak-Derlacz, J. (2015). Integrated sectors - diversified earnings: The (missing) impact of off shoring on wages and wage convergence in the EU27. *Journal of Economic Inequality*. doi:10.1007/s10888-014-9290-y

Patel, P., & Vega M. (1999). Patterns of internationalization of corporate technology: location versus home country advantages. *Research Policy, 28*, 145-155. doi:10.1016/S0048-7333(98)00117-6

Paul, C. J. M., & Yasar, M. (2009). Outsourcing, productivity, and input composition at the plant level. *Canadian Journal of Economic, 42*, 422-439. doi:10.1111/j.1540-5982.2009.01514.x

Penrose, E. T. (1959). *The theory of the growth of the firm.* Bungalore, Karnataka: Indian Institute of Management Bangalore: Edith T. Penrose.

Pisano, G., & Shih, S. (2009). Restoring American competitiveness. *Harvard Business Review*. Retrieved from https://hbr.org/2009/07/restoring-american-competitiveness

Piscitello, L., & Rabbiosi, L. (2006). How does knowledge transfer from foreign subsidiaries affect parent companies' innovative capacity? *Danish Research Unit for Industrial Dynamics (DRUID) Working Papers*, 06-22.

Poppo, L., & Zenger, T. (1998). Testing alternative theories of the firm: transaction cost, knowledge-based, and measurement explanations for make-or-buy decisions in information services. *Strategic Management*

Journal, 19, 853-877. https://dx.doi.org/10.1002/(SICI)1097-0266(199809)19:9<853:AID-SMJ977>3.0.CO;2-B

Porter, M. E. (2008). The five competitive forces. That shape strategy, *Harvard Business Review, 86*(1), 25-40. Retrieved from https://hbr.org/2008/01/the-five-competitive-forces-that-shape-strategy

Porter, M. E., & Jan, W. R. (2012, March). Choosing the United States. *Harvard Business Review (HBR)*. Retrieved from https://hbr.org/2012/03/choosing-the-united-states

Pol, A., Garicano, L., & Rossi-Hansberg, E. (2006). Offshoring in a Knowledge Economy. *Quarterly Journal of Economics, 121*(1), 31–77. doi:10.1093/qje/121.1.31

Prahalad, C. K., & Hamel, G. (1990). The core competence of the corporation. *Harvard Business Review, 68*(3), 79-91. Retrieved from https://hbr.org/1990/05/the-core-competence-of-the-corporation

Qu, Z., & Brocklehurst, M. (2003). What will it take for China to become a competitive force in offshore outsourcing?: An analysis of the role of transaction cost in supplier selection, *Journal of Information Technology, 18*(1), 53-67. doi:10.1080/0268396031000077459

Quinn, J. B., & Hilmer, F. G. (1994). Strategic outsourcing. *Sloan Management Review, 35*(4), 43-55. doi:10.1016/0024-6301(95)00075-5

Quinn, J. B., & Hilmer, F. G. (1994). Strategic outsourcing. *Sloan Management Review, 35*(4), 43-55. Retrieved from https://sloanreview.mit.edu/article/strategic-outsourcing/

Ravishankar, M. N., Cohen, L., & El Sawad, A. (2010). Examining resistance, accommodation, and the pursuit of aspiration in the Indian IT-BPO space: Reflections on two case studies. *Industrial Relations Journal, 41*(2), 154-167. doi:10.1111/j.1468-2338.2009.00560.x

Razzolini, T., & Vannoni, D. (2011). Export Premia and Sub-Contracting Discount. Passive Strategies and Performance in Domestic and Foreign Markets, paper presented at the conference "The International Firm: Access to Finance and Organisational Modes," *Centro Studi Luca D'Agliano, Milan*, 21-22. doi:10.1111/j.1467-9701.2011.01329.x

Reshoring Initiative. (2010). Bringing manufacturing back home. Retrieved from http://www.reshorenow.org/

Reuter, C., Foerstl, K., Hartmann, E., & Blome, C. (2010). Sustainable global supplier management: the role of dynamic capabilities in achieving competitive advantage, *The Journal of Supply Chain Management*, *46*(2), 45-63. doi:10.1111/j.1745-493X.2010.03189.x

Ricart, J., Enright, M., Ghemawat, P., Hart, S., & Khanna, T., (2004). New frontiers in international strategy. *Journal of International Business Studies*, *35*, 175-200. doi:10.1057/palgrave.jibs.8400080

Rilla, N., & Squicciarini, M. (2011). R & D (Re) location and offshore outsourcing: A management perspective. *International Journal of Management Reviews*, *13*, 393-413. doi:10.1111/j.1468-2370.2011.00297.x

Ring, P. S., & Van de Ven, A. H. (1994). Developmental processes of cooperative inter-organizational relationships. *Academy of Management Review*, *19*, 90-118. doi:10.2307/258836

Robertson, C. J., Lamin, A., & Livanis, G. (2010). Stakeholder perceptions of offshoring and outsourcing: The role of embedded Issues. *Journal of Business Ethics*, *95*(2), 167-189. doi:10.1007/s10551-009-0353-0

Robinson, P. K., & Hsieh, L. (2016). Re-shoring: A strategic renewal of luxury clothing supply chains, *Operation Management Review*. Retrieved from http://dx.doi.org/10.1007/s12063-016-0116-x

Rothaermel, F. T., Hitt, M. A., & Jobe, L. A. (2006). Balancing vertical integration and strategic outsourcing: Effects on product portfolio, product success, and firm performance. *Strategic Management Journal*, 27, 1033-1056. doi:10.1002/smj.55

Rousseau, D. M. (1995). *Psychological contracts in organizations: Understanding written and unwritten agreements*. Thousand Oaks, CA: Sage.

Rosario, C. (2009). Offshoring, multinationals, and labour market: A Review of the empirical literature. *Journal of Economic Surveys, 23*(2), 197–249. doi:10.1111/j.1467-6419.2008.00561.x.

Rugman, A. M., Verbeke, A., & Nguyen, Q. T. (2011). Fifty years of international business theory and beyond. *Management International Review*, *51*, 755-786. doi:10.1007/s11575-011-0102-3

Sanchez-Ancochea, K. (2005). Development trajectories and new comparative advantages: Costa Rica and the Dominican Republic under globalization, *World Development, 34*, 996-1015. doi:10.1016/j.worlddev.2005.11.012

Safizadeh, M. H., Field, J. M., & Ritzman, L. P. (2008). Sourcing practices and boundaries of the firm in the financial services industry, *Strategic Management Journal, 29*(1), 79-91. doi:10.1002/smj.641

Saxena, K., & Bharadwaj, S. (2009). Managing business process through outsourcing: A strategic partnering perspective. *Business Process Management Journal, 15*, 687-715. doi:10.1108/14637150910987919

Schuh, C., Kromoser, R., Strohmer, M. F., Pérez, R. R., & Triplat, A. (2009). *The Purchasing Chessboard*™ (pp. 55-207). Berlin Heidelberg, Germany: Springer.

Schwörer T. (2013). Off shoring, domestic outsourcing and productivity: Evidence for a number of European countries. *Review of World Economics, 149*, 131-149. doi:10.1007/s10290-012-0139-9

Sethupathy, G. (2013). Offshoring, wages, and employment: Theory and evidence. *European Economic Review, 62*, 73–97.

Simchi-Levi, D., Peruvankal, J. P., Mulani, N., Read, B., & Ferreira, J. (2012). Is it time to rethink your manufacturing strategy? 0000*Sloan Management Review, 53*(2), 20-22. doi:10.1016/S0022-1996(98)00081-6

Simpson, H. (2012a). How do firms' outward FDI strategies relate to their activity at home? "Empirical evidence for the UK. *The World Economy, 35*, 243-272. doi:10.1111/j.1467-9701.2011.01402.x

Simpson, H. (2012b). Investment abroad and labour adjustment at home: Evidence from UK multinational firms. *Canadian Journal of Economics, 45*, 698-731. doi:10.1111/j.1540-5982.2012.01712.x

Sirkin, H. L., Zinser, M., & Rose, J. (2014, August). *The shifting economics of global manufacturing: How cost competitiveness is changing worldwide.* Boston, MA: Boston Consulting Group.

Slack, N., & Lewis, M. (2002). *Operations strategy.* London, UK: FT Prentice Hall.

Slaughter, M. J. (2000). Production transfer within multinational enterprises and American wages. *Journal of International Economics, 50*, 449-472. doi:10.1016/S0022-1996(98)00081-6

Stehrer, R., Borowiecki, M., Dachs, B., Hanzl-Weiss, D., Kinkel, S., Pöschl, J., Sass, M., Schmall, T. C., & Szalavetz, A. (2012). Global value chains and the EU industry. *WIIW Research Reports no. 383*, Vienna.

Stentoft, J., Olhager, J., Heikkilä, J., & Thoms, L. (2016). Manufacturing backshoring: A systematic literature review. *Operation Management Review*. doi:10.1007/s12063-016- 0110-3

Stringfellow, A., Teagarden, M. B., & Nie, W. (2008). Invisible costs in offshoring services work. *Journal of Operations Management, 26*(2), 164-179. doi:10.1016/j.jom.2007.02.009

Sverke, M., Hellgren, J., & Näswall, K. (2002). No security: A meta-analysis and review of job insecurity and its consequences. *Journal of Occupational Health Psychology, 7*, 242–252. doi:10.1037/1076-8998.7.3.242

Tate, W. L. (2014). Offshoring and reshoring: U.S. insights and research challenges. *Journal of Purchasing and Supply Management, 20*, 66-68. doi:10.1016/j.pursup.2014.01.007

Tate, W. L., & Ellram, L. M. (2009). Offshore outsourcing: A managerial framework. *Journal of Business & Industrial Marketing, 24*(3/4), 256-268. doi:10.1108/08858620910939804

Tate, W. L., Dooley, K. J., &, Ellram, L. M. (2011). Transaction cost and institutional drivers of supplier adoption of environmental practices. *Journal of Business Logistics, 32*(1), 6-16. doi:10.1111/j.2158-1592.2011.01001.x

Tate, W. L., Ellram, L. M., Schoenherr, T., & Petersen, K. J. (2014). Global competitive conditions driving the manufacturing location decision. *Business Horizons, 57*, 381-390. doi:10.1016/j.bushor.2013.12.010

The Organisation for Economic Co-operation and Development (OECD). (2011). *Attractiveness for innovation: Location factors for international investment.* Paris, France: OECD Publishing.

The Organisation for Economic Co-operation and Development (OECD). (2015). *Robots in manufacturing: A first look at the evidence, forthcoming.* Paris, France: OECD Publishing.

The Organisation for Economic Co-operation and Development (OECD). (2013). *OECD-WTO database on trade in value added first estimates*. Retrieved from https://www.oecd.org/sti/ind/TIVA_stats%20 flyer_ENG.pdf

Tomiura, M. (2007). "Foreign outsourcing, exporting, and FDI: A productivity comparison at the firm level". Journal of International Economics #72 (2007) 113–127. doi:10.1016/j.jinteco.2006.11.003

Topalova, P., & Khandelwal, A. (2011). Trade liberalization and firm productivity: The case of India. *The Review of Economics and Statistics, 93*, 995-1009. Retrieved from https://poseidon01.ssrn.com/delivery.php ?ID=166121084101087109014070103064008031005020034052010050028063116022098096051029110011084100017088022066004005040014014115081125013113021098007115002098119072073012100007004027113096031123064098091&EXT=pdf

Trent R. J., & Monczka, R. M. (2003). International purchasing and global sourcing: What are the differences. *Journal of Supply Chain Management, 39*(4), 1–16. https://dx.doi.org/10.1111/j.1745-493X.2003.tb00162.x

Trkman, P. (2010). The critical success factors of business process management. *International Journal of Information Management, 30*(2), 125-134. doi:10.1016/j.ijinfomgt.2009.07.003

van Welsum, D. (2004). *In search of 'offshoring': Evidence from U.S. imports of services*. London, UK: Birkbeck College, mimeo.

Vagadia, B. (2012). *Strategic outsourcing*. London, UK: Springer.

Van Knippenberg, D., & van Schie, E. C. M. (2000). Foci and correlates of organizational identification. *Journal of Occupational and Organizational Psychology, 73*(2), 137–148. doi:10.1348/096317900166949

Veltri, N. F., Saunders, C. S., & Kavan, C. B. (2008). Information systems back sourcing: Correcting problems and responding to opportunities. *California Management Review, 51*(1), 50-76. doi:10.2307/41166468

Veugelers, R. (1997). Internal R&D expenditures and external technology sourcing. *Research Policy, 26*, 303-315. doi:10.5465/ame.1992.4274302

Weil, D. (2014). *The fissured workplace: Why work became so bad for so many and what can be done to improve it*. Boston, MA: Harvard University Press.

Welch J. A., & Nayak P. R. (1992). Strategic sourcing: A progressive approach to the make or buy decision. *Academy of Management Executive, 6*(1), 23-30. doi:10.14254/2071-8330.2015/8-1/4

Wiesmann, B., Hilletofth, P., Snoei, J.R., & Erikson, D. (2017). Drivers and barriers to reshoring: a literature review on offshoring in reverse. *European Business Review, 29*(1),15-42. doi:10.1108/EBR-03-2016-0050

Whitfield, G. (2017). Offshoring, overshoring, and reshoring: The long-term effects of manufacturing decisions in the United States. *Breaking up the Global Value Chain (Advances in International Management, Vol. 30), Emerald Publishing Limited,* 123-139. doi:10.1108

Willcocks, L., Hindle, J., Feeny, D., & Lacity, M. (2004) IT and business process outsourcing: The knowledge potential. *Information System Management, 21*(3), 7-15. doi:10.1201/1078/44432.21.3.20040601/82471.2

Williamson, O. E. (1985). *The Economic institutions of capitalism.* New York, NY: The Free Press.

Williamson, O. E. (1996). *Mechanisms of governance.* New York, NY: Oxford University Press.

Williamson, O. E. (2008), Outsourcing: Transaction cost economics and supply chain management*. *Journal of Supply Chain Management, 44,* 5-16. doi:10.1111/j.1745-493X.2008.00051.x

Wolszczak-Derlacz, J., & Parteka, A. (2015). Does off shoring affect industry employment?: Evidence from a wide European panel of countries. *Journal of International Studies, 8*(1), 41-52. doi:10.14254/2071-8330.2015/8-1/4

World Trade Organization (WTO). (2007). *Globalization, offshoring and jobs.* Retrieved from https://www.wto.org/

World Trade Organization (WTO). (2011). *Globalization, offshoring, and jobs.* Retrieved from https://www.wto.org/

Zimmermann, A., Raab, K., & Zanotelli, L. (2012). Vicious and virtuous circles of offshoring attitudes and relational behaviours: A configurational study of German IT developers. *Information Systems Journal, 23*(1), 65–88. doi:10.1111/j.1365-2575.2012.00399

ABOUT THE AUTHOR

Dr. Ivan Salaberrios resides in Pickerington, Ohio. Dr. Ivan holds several accredited degrees; a Bachelor of Technical management Science (BS) in Management from DeVry University; a Master of Business Administration (MBA) from Keller Graduate School; and a Doctor of Business Administration (DBA) from Walden University. Dr. Ivan also is a certified Project Management Professional (PMP) and Lean Six Sigma Black Belt Certified.

Dr. Ivan is the CEO and founder of AIM Technical Consultants. His career in the telecommunications industry began as a field engineer working with AMPs Radio Equipment, where he obtained extensive experience in RF Engineering, Network Engineering and Project Management.

In 17 years, Dr. Ivan has grown AIM from a handful of engineers to one of the largest staffing and engineering firms focused exclusively in wireless telecom. This growth is largely attributable to Ivan's relationship-building skills, dedication to exceptional service delivery, and unwavering focus on continuous improvement. Dr. Ivan is a Gulf War veteran, serving an enlistment term in the US Navy on the USS Yorktown CG-48. He was honorably discharged in 1992.

To reach Dr. Ivan Salaberrios for information on consulting or doctoral coaching, please **e-mail:** ivans@aimtechinc.com

ABOUT THE COMPANY

AIM Technical Consultants has experienced significant wireless industry growth since opening for business in 1999. We attribute this proven track record to our ability to consistently deliver IT field management and wireless technology implementation, allowing our customers peace of mind. Add to that our dedication to providing the best technical and professional services in the industry and AIM Technical Consultant's commitment to positioning ourselves as the *go to* wireless industry service provider, and the results speak for themselves. AIM Technical provides services in IT and wireless telecommunications committed to delivering unparalleled Cloud Engineering life-cycle support to our demanding customers with specific IT and wireless telecommunication needs.

For more information, please contact **email:** office@aimtechnical.com **phone:** 614-452-773 **website:** https://www.aimtechnical.com/

Made in the USA
Monee, IL
19 November 2024

70532146R00105